THE EVERYTHING

EASY LARGE-PRINT
CROSSWORDS BOOK, VOLUME VI

Dear Reader,

I didn't create these crossword puzzles to stump you.
These are nice puzzles designed to make you feel good.
That's because they're easy, but not *too* easy. You'll still
need to think. And that's good for your brain. Your neu-
rons will light up with happiness every time you fill in a
word. For me, solving crossword puzzles is a great way
to relax and sharpen the mind.

I've had the pleasure of creating dozens of puzzle
books. It was a joy putting this one together for you. We
printed these pages with large print because bigger letters are better. They make the puzzles easier on the eyes
and more fun for the brain.

So if you're looking for puzzles that are completely baf-
fling, then this book probably isn't for you. For everyone
else—grab a pencil, turn the page, and engage your
brain. Let's have some fun!

Charles Timmerman

Welcome to the EVERYTHING® Series!

These handy, accessible books give you all you need to tackle a difficult project, gain a new hobby, comprehend a fascinating topic, prepare for an exam, or even brush up on something you learned back in school but have since forgotten.

You can choose to read an Everything® book from cover to cover or just pick out the information you want from our four useful boxes: e-questions, e-facts, e-alerts, and e-ssentials. We give you everything you need to know on the subject, but throw in a lot of fun stuff along the way, too.

We now have more than 400 Everything® books in print, spanning such wide-ranging categories as weddings, pregnancy, cooking, music instruction, foreign language, crafts, pets, New Age, and so much more. When you're done reading them all, you can finally say you know Everything®!

PUBLISHER Karen Cooper

MANAGING EDITOR, EVERYTHING® SERIES Lisa Laing

COPY CHIEF Casey Ebert

ASSISTANT PRODUCTION EDITOR Alex Guarco

ACQUISITIONS EDITOR Lisa Laing

EVERYTHING® SERIES COVER DESIGNER Erin Alexander

Visit the entire Everything® series at *www.everything.com*

THE EVERYTHING® EASY LARGE-PRINT CROSSWORDS BOOK

VOLUME VI

More than 100 easy crossword
puzzles in large print

Charles Timmerman
Founder of Funster.com

Adams Media
New York London Toronto Sydney New Delhi

Adams Media
An Imprint of Simon & Schuster, Inc.
100 Technology Center Drive
Stoughton, MA 02072

An Everything® Series Book.
Everything® and everything.com® are registered trademarks of Simon & Schuster, Inc.

For information about special discounts for bulk purchases, please contact Simon & Schuster Special Sales at 1-866-506-1949 or business@simonandschuster.com.

The Simon & Schuster Speakers Bureau can bring authors to your live event. For more information or to book an event contact the Simon & Schuster Speakers Bureau at 1-866-248-3049 or visit our website at www.simonspeakers.com.

Manufactured in the United States of America

16 2024

Library of Congress Cataloging-in-Publication Data has been applied for.

ISBN 978-1-4405-7157-2

Dedicated to
Suzanne, Calla, and Meryl.

Acknowledgments

I would like to thank each and every one of the more than half a million people who have visited my website, *www.funster.com*, to play word games and puzzles. You have shown me how much fun puzzles can be and how addictive they can become!

It is a pleasure to acknowledge the folks at Adams Media who made this book possible. I particularly want to thank my editor, Lisa Laing, for so skillfully managing the many projects we have worked on together.

Contents

Introduction

What do Rosa Parks, Richard Nixon, Jesse Owens, and crossword puzzles have in common? They were all born in the year 1913. In that year, a journalist named Arthur Wynne published a "word-cross" puzzle in the *New York World*'s Sunday newspaper. Though it was diamond-shaped, it had all of the features of the crossword puzzles that we know and love today. The name evolved into *crossword* as the paper continued to publish the popular word puzzles.

It wasn't until 1924 that the first book of crossword puzzles was published. That was when the crossword craze really began. It joined other fads of the Roaring Twenties like goldfish-swallowing, flagpole sitting, yo-yos, and pogo sticks. Of course, not all of these fads survived (perhaps fortunately).

Besides crossword puzzles, some really beautiful things came out of the 1920s. In music, jazz surged in popularity and George Gershwin's *Rhapsody in Blue* was performed for the first time. In literature, F. Scott Fitzgerald published some of his most enduring novels, including *The Great Gatsby*. In design, it was the beginning of art deco. That's how the world was shifting when crossword puzzles came of age.

Crossword puzzles became popular closer to a time when entertainment required *active* participation. In those days, people actually played sports rather than watched them, told each other stories rather than turning on the television, and even sang songs rather than listening to an MP3. Like entertainment of yesteryear, crossword puzzles require your active participation. And this is a refreshing change for those of us who still enjoy a mental workout.

Today, nearly every major newspaper runs a crossword puzzle. Entire sections of bookstores are devoted to crossword puzzle books. (Thanks for choosing this one!) Indeed, crosswords are the most common word puzzle in the world.

Why do crossword puzzles continue to be so popular? Only you can answer that question, since there are as many reasons to work a crossword puzzle as there are solvers. But perhaps it has something to do with the convenient marriage of fun and learning that crossword puzzles offer.

Puzzles

ACROSS

1. Open-and-___ case
5. Recedes
9. Sound of discomfort
12. Muck
13. Hired thug
14. Boo-hoo
15. Womb mate?
16. Used up
17. Mustache site
18. Citrus drinks, for short
20. Open-mouthed
22. Be crazy about
25. "I ___ Ike"
27. "Mad ___" (Mel Gibson movie)
28. Singer Celine
30. Steals from
34. Aviated
36. Director's "Stop!"
37. SWM part
38. Talking bird
39. Pottery oven
41. Campaign (for)
42. Singer Marvin
44. Assail
46. 11- or 12-year-old
49. Hardly strict
50. ___ Tin Tin (old TV dog)
51. Like printers' fingers
54. "Back in Black" band
58. AMEX alternative
59. Roger Bannister's distance
60. Sandwich spread
61. High-speed connection
62. Street shaders
63. Erupt

DOWN

1. Pub crawler
2. "___ do you do?"
3. Commando weapon
4. Voice below alto
5. Roe
6. Halloween word
7. ___ voyage party
8. Proceed on tiptoe
9. West Coast sch.
10. Tight hold
11. Overpublicize
19. ___ Bartlet, president on "The West Wing"
21. ___ of an idea
22. Kind of radio
23. Tyne of "Cagney & Lacey"
24. Beasts in yokes
25. Nephew of Donald Duck
26. Part of IHOP: abbr.
29. Totally gross
31. Boat propellers
32. Like a clear sky
33. Mailed

35. Salary

40. Wizards and Magic org.

43. Japanese cartoon style

45. Midterms and finals

46. Trampled

47. Ingenuity

48. SASE, e.g.

49. Caustic solutions

52. Zero

53. Airline to Holland

55. Spending limit

56. Easter egg application

57. Mooer

Solution on Page 300

ACROSS

1. Blighted urban area
5. Give this for that
9. Tiger Woods's org.
12. "Purple ___" (Jimi Hendrix song)
13. Heavy book
14. Clip-___ (certain sunglasses)
15. "We Try Harder" company
16. Unskilled worker
17. Perry Mason's field
18. Give a hard time
20. Truman who wrote "Breakfast at Tiffany's"
22. "Lawrence of Arabia" star
24. You-know-___
27. Kind of rally
28. Woodcutting tools
32. Per person
34. Perimeter
36. Knotted neckwear
37. Computer memory measure
38. Horse that's had it
40. Kitten's cry
41. Regret deeply
44. Hype
47. Goings-on
52. Idiot boxes
53. SeaWorld performer
55. ___ song (cheaply)
56. Earl Grey for one
57. Authoritative decree
58. ___ Lee of Marvel Comics
59. Meddle
60. Vocal pitch
61. Blockheads

DOWN

1. Ayatollah's predecessor
2. Volcano's output
3. Israeli guns
4. Sloppy condition
5. Heaven's gatekeeper
6. Wednesday's child is full of it
7. Oil company that merged with BP
8. Word before code or colony
9. Prince Charles's sport
10. Member of a pesky swarm
11. "Even ___ speak"
19. Cut off, as branches
21. Termite, e.g.
23. Share one's views
24. Part of WWW
25. Manger contents
26. Columbus Day's mo.
29. Point a gun
30. Minuscule
31. Opposite of NNE
33. Aid
35. Authoritative order
39. Sporty Pontiac

42. Like an eagle in flight

43. Novelist Puzo

44. URL starter

45. Eggs ___ easy

46. Anthem starter

48. In that case

49. ___ care in the world

50. Steffi of tennis

51. Without

54. Campbell's container

Solution on Page 300

ACROSS

1. ___-night doubleheader
4. High or elementary: abbr.
7. "Duck ___" (Marx Brothers film)
11. Blushing
12. Pod veggies
14. Employ
15. In ___ (occupied)
16. The "I" in MIT: abbr.
17. Tech. college major
18. Be extraordinary
21. Like Abner
22. Brit. fliers
23. Parade spoiler
25. "The best is ___ to come!"
26. Corp. honcho
29. Gives the go-ahead
30. Mass confusion
32. Trio before "O"
33. Belfry denizen
34. "All systems go"
35. Kismet
36. Quaker morsel
37. Spot on a playing card
38. Unpretentious
43. Greet from a distance
44. Words before arms or smoke
45. "The Facts of Life" actress Charlotte
47. Lena or Ken of film
48. Flex
49. Everything
50. Classic sneakers
51. Cultural funding gp.
52. Qt. halves

DOWN

1. Capote, to friends
2. Toward the sunset
3. Utopian
4. Hawker's pitch
5. Penny
6. Food that's slung
7. Grain bundle
8. Sty sound
9. Prod
10. Part of mph
13. Home music system
19. Cousins and such
20. Andrew Lloyd Webber smash
23. Filch
24. Alias
25. Have a gabfest
26. Nonsense
27. CPR provider
28. Early afternoon hour
30. "Misery" costar James
31. Sociable soaking spot
35. Tree with cones
36. Country singer Buck

37. Bamboo eater

38. Carnegie or Evans

39. "The Art of Love" poet

40. Dentist's request

41. Mozart's "a"

42. "Stop right there!"

43. Moo goo gai pan pan

46. Golfer Ernie

Solution on Page 300

ACROSS

1. Duck for apples
4. Bell and Barker
7. Prima donna
11. Abner adjective
12. Discharge
14. Kiln
15. Stretchables
17. Proof of ownership
18. Wedding helpers
19. Warm embrace
21. "Wow!"
22. All thumbs
25. Llama country
28. Med. diagnostic tool
29. It's flipped in anger
31. Stunt rider Knievel
32. PC screen
33. Part in a play
34. Letterman dental feature
35. Doorway welcomer
36. Memo-heading abbr.
37. Renewable energy type
39. Q–U connectors
41. Keep an ___ to the ground
42. Plaza Hotel girl of fiction
46. Meat inspection org.
49. Got one's bearings
51. Word before ring or swing
52. Something to whistle
53. Silly-Putty holder
54. Line of rotation
55. Dose amt.
56. Memorial Day month

DOWN

1. ___ cheese dressing
2. Removes a squeak from
3. Ho-hum
4. ___-Goldwyn-Mayer
5. Some of the Pennsylvania Dutch
6. "Attack!" to Rover
7. Jump out of the way
8. "___ Got You Under My Skin"
9. Peace sign shape
10. In addition
13. All I got was this lousy ___
16. Capital of South Korea
20. Prefix for corn or verse
23. Parcel of land
24. Pinball infraction
25. Tent pin
26. Tanguay and Gabor
27. "___ Man" (1984 Estevez film)
28. "The A-Team" star
30. TV room
32. Rabbit's treat
33. Boca ___, FL
35. Calf's call
38. Clues, to a detective

Puzzle 4

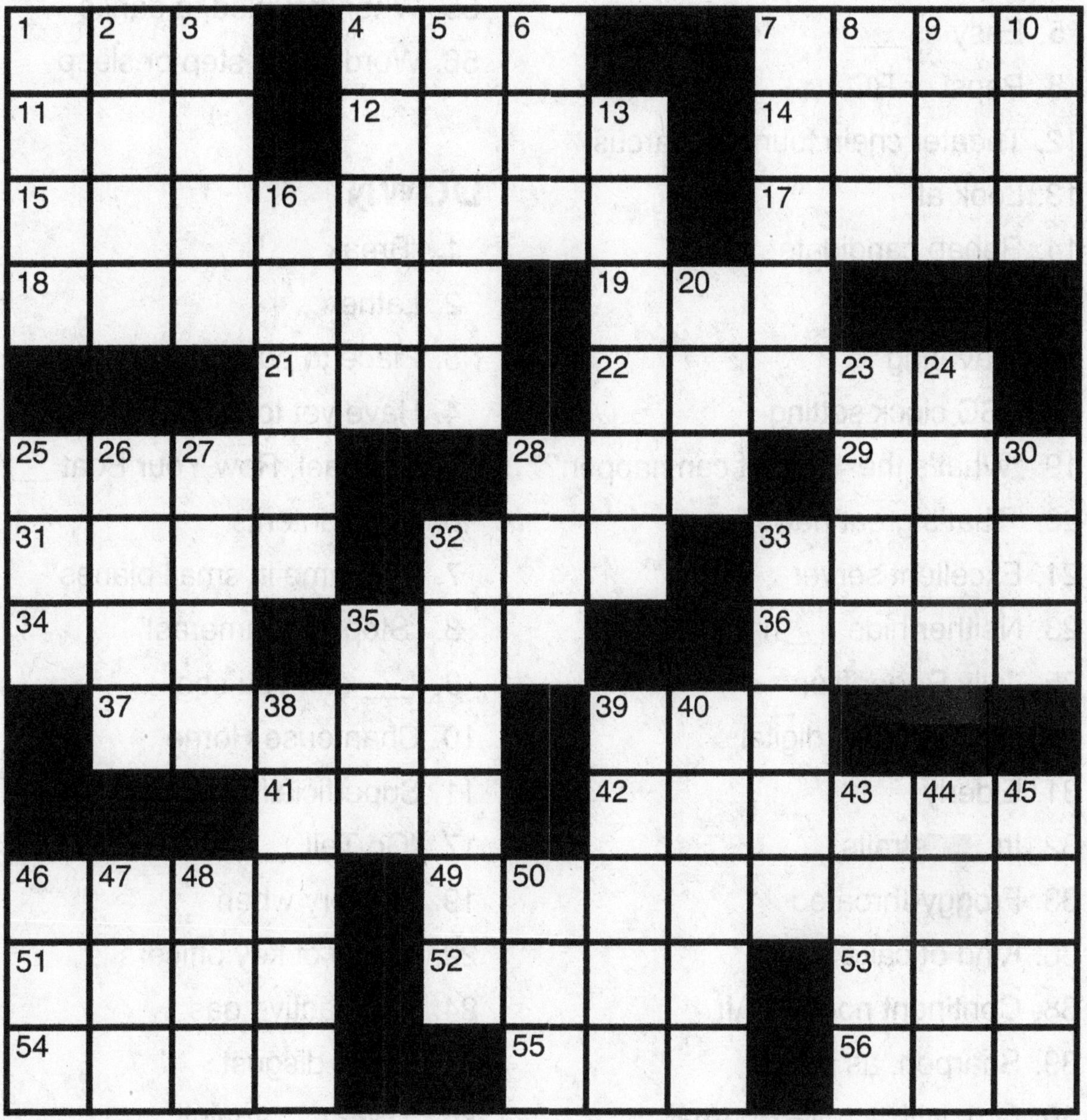

39. Jockey's handful
40. Catch some Zs
43. Unit on a list
44. Company whose mascot is Sonic the Hedgehog
45. Nervously irritable
46. Thurman of Hollywood
47. Chi-Town team
48. "___ look like a mind reader?"
50. Dirt road depression

Solution on Page 300

ACROSS

1. 60s hairdo
5. Easy as ___
8. Pepsi or RC
12. Theater chain founder Marcus
13. Look at
14. Rehab candidate
15. Ill at ___
16. Wavering
18. BBC clock setting
19. "What's the ___ that can happen?"
20. "That's great news!"
21. Excellent server
23. Neither hide ___ hair
25. Jolly Roger flier
27. Alternative to digital
31. Elderly
32. In ___ straits
33. Froggy-throated
36. Kind of cake
38. Continent north of Afr.
39. Sharpen, as skills
40. Org. with a noted journal
43. Famous
45. Luke, to Darth
48. Reverend
50. Actress Thompson of "Howards End"
51. Skipped town
52. AOL or MSN
53. Some soda containers
54. Kitten cries
55. When doubled, a dance
56. Words after step or sleep

DOWN

1. "Break ___!"
2. Lather
3. Place to pull over
4. Have yet to pay
5. "Michael, Row Your Boat ___"
6. Keg contents
7. Big name in small planes
8. "Stop the cameras!"
9. "___ can you see . . ."
10. Chanteuse Horne
11. Superficially cultured
17. "Go Tell ___ the Mountain"
19. Slippery when ___
22. Group of key officers
24. Radioactive gas
25. Cry of disgust
26. "Here ___ again!"
28. Football official
29. Assn.
30. "I didn't know that!"
34. Phoenix's NBA team
35. X-rated
36. Mount Everest guide
37. Seed case

40. Radio letters

41. 5,280 feet

42. All over again

44. New age composer John

46. Prefix with potent or present

47. Political cartoonist Thomas

49. Doorkeepers' demands, briefly

50. Prefix with sphere or system

Solution on Page 301

ACROSS

1. Clumsy sort
4. Like centenarians
7. Campus bigwig
11. Epcot's home
12. "Don't ___ fool!"
13. Moulin ___
14. Kind of shot
15. Took a chair
16. See eye to eye
17. ___ Luis Obispo
18. Funnyman Foxx
20. Leia's love
22. Code-breaking org.
23. "The Wizard of Oz" studio
26. Speakers' pause fillers
28. Kathmandu resident
31. "Live Free or Die," for New Hampshire
34. Forbidden acts
35. Van Gogh subjects
37. Tubes
38. Easy letters?
39. Golfing standard
41. Margarine container
44. Funeral fire
45. Data-sharing syst.
47. Acquire, as a debt
51. Strike caller
53. Fight stopper, briefly
54. Flowery verse
55. Squeezing snake
56. Bygone car
57. Big-eyed birds
58. Supply with weapons
59. Biblical transport

DOWN

1. Slays, mob-style
2. To whom a Muslim prays
3. Animal life
4. Baby docs, briefly
5. Gets smart
6. Goes out with
7. Hound
8. Ger. continent
9. Get better, as wine
10. Born as
13. Slangy wonderful
19. Dapper ___
21. Cashews and such
23. "___ overboard!"
24. Mop & ___ (floor cleaner)
25. Prefix with "understanding"
27. One of the Stooges
29. Part of SASE
30. Newsgroup message
31. Hamm of soccer
32. Planet, poetically
33. Quirky habit

36. Snoop

37. Quake aftershock

40. Caribbean resort island

42. The "U" of UHF

43. Bread maker

44. Be nosy

46. Cranny's companion

47. Stock debut, for short

48. This instant

49. Cartoon collectible

50. ___ Constitution

52. Nonstick cooking spray

Solution on Page 301

ACROSS

1. Old Soviet news agency
5. Course for new immigrants: abbr.
8. SSE's opposite
11. Eject, as lava
12. Marks of Zorro
14. Boat mover
15. Look (over)
16. Prego rival
17. School org.
18. ___ Allan Poe
20. Prepare, as tea
22. Forty-___ (gold rush participant)
24. Morse bit
25. Nonsensical
26. Like Abe
29. Pea container
30. "Here Comes the ___"
31. Partner of abet
33. Prepare leftovers
36. Seven-___ cake
38. "Monsters, ___"
39. Old piano key material
40. F. ___ Fitzgerald
43. Spotless
45. Chinese cookware
46. Online auction site
48. Mary's fleecy follower
51. Doctors' org.
52. Deception
53. Wild time
54. Mom's month
55. Dorm overseers, for short
56. "What's in a ___?," said Juliet

DOWN

1. Cooking meas.
2. GI's address
3. Suitor's song
4. Bjorn Borg's homeland
5. Book before Nehemiah
6. Char
7. Knee's place
8. Opposite of "yup"
9. Basketball Hall-of-Famer Archibald
10. Prepare presents
13. ___ B. Anthony
19. Test for coll. seniors
21. "That'll be ___ day!"
22. Small drink of liquor
23. "Are you ___ out?"
24. Mafia boss
26. Humble home
27. Japanese farewell
28. Top-___ (best)
30. Baglike structure
32. Arid
34. Box-office smash
35. Go in

36. Big fib

37. Frankie of "Beach Blanket Bingo"

40. Did laps in a pool

41. Unwakeable state

42. Give the thumbs-up

43. Acapulco abode

44. Caustic compounds

47. Prickly husk

49. "Grand Hotel" studio

50. See ya

Solution on Page 301

ACROSS

1. Uno + dos
5. Stadium cheers
9. Educ. institution
12. Arizona Indian
13. Working without ___
14. Attention-getting shout
15. Elec. company, e.g.
16. Hearts or darts
17. Calculate sums
18. Magnum ___: great work
20. "Me and Bobby ___"
22. Nonchalant
25. Grp. putting on shows for troops
26. Balloon filler
27. Surgery souvenir
30. Hold
34. Caribbean music
35. Midsection
37. One step ___ time
38. Movie locations
40. Pierce with a fork
41. "Frasier" network
42. Used a stool
44. Singers Hall and ___
46. Fancy goodbye
49. ___ the fat
51. All you ___ eat
52. Run the country
54. Sounds from pounds
58. Banned pesticide
59. They worshipped from ___
60. Meg of "In the Cut"
61. Top of the corp. ladder
62. Amount between all and none
63. Start a card game

DOWN

1. Thanksgiving, e.g.: abbr.
2. Undergo decomposition
3. Prefix with dermal
4. Farm storage structures
5. Pasta sauce maker
6. Collections of anecdotes
7. Skirt edge
8. Wineglass features
9. Thick carpet
10. Surrender
11. London's ___ Park
19. Exterminator's target
21. Gear part
22. Lowest voice
23. Find attractive
24. Smell ___ (be suspicious)
25. ___ Major (the Big Dipper)
28. Price paid
29. ___ deco
31. Diatribe
32. Can ___ true?
33. Campaign funders, for short
36. A woodwind

39. Reverse of NNW
43. Surrounding glows
45. Oscar or Tony
46. "Back in Black" rock band
47. Florida's Miami-___ County
48. Put ___ words
49. Oyster relative
50. Roll call reply

53. ET carrier
55. Deli loaf
56. Air safety org.
57. Eddie Murphy's old show, for short

Solution on Page 301

ACROSS

1. Speedometer meas.
4. Mind-reading ability, for short
7. Burn with hot liquid
12. XXX counterpart
13. Descriptive wd.
14. Soprano Callas
15. Payroll ID
16. Bro's relative
17. "___ and Ivory"
18. Wee
20. Touches down
21. Solo in "Star Wars"
23. "___ in the Family"
24. Lounge
27. Have in hand
29. Full of breezes
33. Slippery tree
34. Coffee order: abbr.
35. Neckline shape
36. TV's warrior princess
38. NNW's reverse
39. Emeralds and diamonds
40. Compete (for)
42. ___ Tafari (Haile Selassie)
44. Place to wash up
47. Speeder spotter
51. Cuban boat boy González
52. "___ to Joy"
54. "What was ___ do?"
55. Actor Nick
56. ___ Tin Tin (heroic dog of 1950s TV)
57. Speeder stopper
58. Discourage from proceeding
59. "Wanna ___?"
60. 180 degrees from WSW

DOWN

1. A majority
2. Model
3. Sharpen, as a knife
4. High mark with low effort
5. High-tech weapons prog.
6. Nightwear, briefly
7. Aroma
8. Jewish mystical doctrine
9. Elvis Presley's middle name
10. Jenny, "The Swedish Nightingale"
11. Calendar boxes
19. Gretzky's grp.
22. Like Leif Ericson
23. Hot temper
24. "Superman" villain Luthor
25. Bullring cheer
26. K–O filler
28. Craven of horror
30. "If ___ told you once . . ."
31. Sleep acronym
32. Aye

1	2	3		4	5	6		7	8	9	10	11
12				13				14				
15				16				17				
18			19						20			
		21		22		23						
24	25	26			27	28			29	30	31	32
33				34						35		
36			37		38				39			
		40	41				42	43				
44	45	46						47		48	49	50
51					52	53			54			
55					56				57			
58					59				60			

37. Fly a plane
39. Fed. property overseer
41. Kind of circle or tube
43. "___ You Glad You're You?"
44. Curve
45. Skin soother
46. Sediment

48. Casino cubes
49. ". . . hit me like ___ of bricks"
50. Piece of rodeo gear
52. Sun or moon
53. Tool and ___

Solution on Page 302

ACROSS

1. Billy Joel's "___ to Extremes"
4. Provide weapons for
7. Salon job
11. "___ 'til You Drop"
12. "Just ___," the Nike slogan
14. Part of U.S.A.: abbr.
15. Do the floor
16. WWII turning point
17. Unconscious state
18. Skin openings
20. Thick-skinned critter
22. Flanders of "The Simpsons"
23. Angler's need
24. Bake-off figure
26. TLC givers
27. "FRONTLINE" airer
30. Baseball score
31. Glasgow residents
33. Trigger's rider
34. "You ain't seen nothin' ___!"
35. Prefix with cycle or angle
36. College official
37. Donkey pin-on
38. Same old grind
39. Trap
41. Like a beaver
43. ___ tube (television set)
44. Paper quantity
46. Short sleep
48. Matinee hero
49. Belgrade resident
50. Baden-Baden, e.g.
51. ___ of one's existence
52. Day___ (fluorescent paint brand)
53. Computer key: abbr.

DOWN

1. ThinkPad developer
2. Sticky stuff
3. Foe
4. Threw in
5. Fishing poles
6. ABBA's "Mamma ___"
7. Silently understood
8. "___ Fire," the Springsteen hit
9. Pixar fish
10. "La la" preceder
13. Despot
19. NBA official
21. Snake's sound
23. Oven setting
24. Hue's partner
25. Clamor
27. False appearance
28. Constrictor
29. Prefix for thesis
31. Constellation component
32. Town shouters
36. Used a shovel

30

37. Billiards furniture

38. "First Blood" character

39. Carbonated drink

40. Midday

41. Husband of a countess

42. Emulates Eminem

43. Baby's dinner wear

45. Brain wave reading: abbr.

47. Cal.'s ocean

Solution on Page 302

ACROSS

1. Poorly lit
4. Best toys in the whirl?
8. George Gershwin's brother
11. ___ Mountains: Europe/Asia border range
13. Cry of pain
14. Lancelot's title
15. Dust Bowl migrant
16. "___ long way to Tipperary"
17. "Scent ___ Woman"
18. Actor Kilmer
20. "Water Lilies" painter Claude
22. Place to sit
25. Half a ticket
27. Online shorthand in reply to a joke
28. Trucker with a transmitter
30. Acerbic
34. Suitable
35. Soup go-with
37. "Gimme ___!" (Indiana cheerleaders' cry)
38. "___, right!" ("I bet!")
40. Bullets
41. Waiter's payoff
42. ___ Minor (constellation)
44. Prices
46. Whooping ___
49. NNE's opposite
50. Vert. counterpart, on old TVs
51. High point

54. Countrywide: abbr.
58. Wedding vow
59. After-bath wear
60. Sow chow
61. Just off the assembly line
62. Practice boxing
63. Printer's widths

DOWN

1. Half a quartet
2. Tick off
3. Chiang ___ (Thai city)
4. "Double, double, ___ and trouble . . ."
5. Over's partner
6. Dell or Toshiba products, for short
7. SeaWorld whale
8. "Help ___ the way!"
9. In abundance
10. "I smell ___"
12. Denim pioneer Strauss
19. Circular segments
21. Out-of-date: abbr.
22. Potter's medium
23. Bob of "Road" films
24. Claudia ___ Taylor (Lady Bird Johnson)
25. 1965 Alabama march site
26. Cable car
29. Sheep cries
31. Quaker ___
32. Moon ___ Zappa

33. Steals, with "off"

36. Physicians, briefly

39. Attila, for one

43. Raises, as children

45. Holds the deed to

46. Goatee's place

47. Was a passenger

48. And pretty maids all in ___

49. Clairvoyant

52. Radar gun aimer

53. CEO's degree, maybe

55. Ginger ___ (Canada Dry product)

56. Actor Selleck

57. '60s records

Solution on Page 302

ACROSS

1. Contingencies
4. Barn birds
8. Speed meas.
11. Legume
13. And it ___ to pass . . .
14. Whitney or Yale
15. I never ___ man I didn't like (Will Rogers)
16. Prong of a fork
17. "Here's ___ in your eye"
18. Coin opening
20. Bullwinkle, for one
22. Build on
25. Tongue-clucking sound
26. Mai ___ (rum cocktail)
27. Turn tail
30. Junior-to-be
34. Bullring shout
35. NBC morning show
37. Hawaiian garland
38. Cylindrical pasta
40. Subterfuge
41. .
42. U-turn from SSW
44. Property claims
46. Astronaut's milieu
49. Dance in a grass skirt
51. Access the Internet, with "on"
52. Hasn't ___ to stand on
54. Church service
58. Mattel card game
59. Train track part
60. Bldg. units
61. Ryan of "When Harry Met Sally"
62. Surprisingly lively
63. "___ up or shut up!"

DOWN

1. Big Blue
2. Doctor's charge
3. Warmed the bench
4. Bi-, quadrupled
5. "Just a sec!"
6. "K–O" connection
7. "What ___ to be the problem?"
8. Short note
9. +
10. Take cover
12. Magazine publisher Condé
19. Hay storage place
21. Approves
22. From ___ (the gamut)
23. Surrealist Salvador
24. Weight-loss plan
25. Oolong and pekoe
28. Traditional tales
29. End of some e-mail addresses
31. Ye ___ Curiosity Shoppe
32. Lowly worker
33. Chart toppers

34

36. Raise one's voice

39. Ltd., here

43. Approaches

45. "___ Rock" (Simon & Garfunkel hit)

46. Urban renewal target

47. Fried corn bread

48. Obviously eager

49. One named in a will

50. Hideous

53. Drink like a dog

55. PC program, briefly

56. VW predecessors?

57. Retired fast plane: abbr.

Solution on Page 302

ACROSS

1. Start of a magician's cry
5. Washroom: abbr.
8. Use a shovel
11. New Mexico art community
12. Filet of ___
13. Clean air org.
14. Run ___ (go wild)
15. Twerp
16. High tennis shot
17. Knight's lady
18. Gun a motor
19. Lends a hand to
20. Trouble
22. Long, long time
24. Family docs
27. B-ball official
29. Change with the times
33. Bogey beater
34. Up, in baseball
36. Hosp. diagnostic
37. Liability's opposite
39. ___ liebe dich
40. Antonym's antonym: abbr.
41. Put in stitches
43. String after "Q"
45. Ship pole
48. Cable movie channel
50. There are 435 in Cong.
54. "The Name of the Rose" author
    Umberto

55. Sheepish sounds
56. "Beverly Hills Cop" character Foley
57. Camera type, briefly
58. ___ Well that Ends . . .
59. Falafel bread
60. Take legal action
61. Rep.'s rival
62. Soup of a sort

DOWN

1. Just slightly
2. Football's Crimson Tide, for short
3. ___ and board
4. Cockeyed
5. "St. Elmo's Fire" actor Rob
6. ___ and kicking
7. Nov. 11 honoree
8. Sandwich shop
9. Digital music player
10. Chews the fat
12. "Sesame ___"
19. "___ away we go!"
21. Speechify
23. Solemn pledges
24. No. on a transcript
25. Mas' mates
26. Last year's jrs.
28. J. Edgar Hoover's org.
30. Pro-___ (some tourneys)
31. Use a crowbar
32. Sn, chemically speaking

Puzzle 13

35. Horizontally
38. Approximate no.
42. Blubber source
44. Snares
45. Disorder
46. Civil rights org.
47. Achy
49. Soothing ointment
51. Lighted sign over a door
52. Sampras or Rose
53. Shredded side dish
55. No good

Solution on Page 303

ACROSS

1. Word repeated before "pants on fire"
5. OR personnel
8. "___ Slidin' Away"
12. "What'll ___?" (bartender's question)
13. "Shut yer ___!"
14. "Go, ___!"
15. Carve in stone
16. New Year's ___
17. $20 bill dispensers
18. Bubbly beverage
19. "Return of the Jedi" creature
21. Actor Affleck
24. Exterminator's targets
28. Ryder Cup org.
31. The "L" of XXL
34. Mauna ___
35. Howard of "Happy Days"
36. Chinese or Japanese
37. All systems go
38. Take nourishment
39. Call up
40. Rushmore and Rainier: abbr.
41. One-pot dinners
43. College sr.'s test
45. Get better, as a cut
48. Labor Day mo.
52. Burrowing mammal
55. Rainey and Barker
57. Glacial
58. Not quite closed
59. Hosp. area for acute conditions
60. Prefix with dynamic
61. "___ forgive our debtors"
62. It's south of SD
63. ___ St. Laurent

DOWN

1. Whoppers
2. "Leave ___ Beaver"
3. "Alphabet Song" start
4. Get-well program
5. Colorant
6. Glowing review
7. Gush forth
8. Vampire vanquisher
9. The Beatles' "___ It Be"
10. "___ a Rock" by Simon & Garfunkel
11. U.K. leaders
20. First game of the season
22. Pass, as time
23. Partner of Crosby and Stills
25. Grand ___
26. Tugboat sound
27. Fifth Avenue landmark
28. JFK or LBJ
29. Capricorn's symbol
30. Poker starter

32. "___ Lobo" (John Wayne film)

33. Crips or Bloods

42. . . . ___ angels fear to tread

44. High-school composition

46. Ugandan dictator

47. "Arsenic and Old ___"

49. Height: abbr.

50. Tiny skin opening

51. Pairs

52. Lamb's bleat

53. Breakfast drinks, for short

54. Murphy's ___

56. Undersea prowler

Solution on Page 303

ACROSS

1. Gas-additive letters
4. Julia of "The Addams Family"
8. "The Simpsons" girl
12. CBS logo
13. Austen heroine
14. Memo abbr.
15. Tax mo.
16. Wing measurement
17. Electronics giant
18. ___ tell you something . . .
20. President Lincoln
22. Money owed
25. Cravings
29. Soviet news source
32. Circle parts
34. Car co. bought by Chrysler
35. "___ kleine Nachtmusik"
36. Fluffy scarf
37. Lifetime Oscar winner Kazan
38. Second Amendment advocacy gp.
39. Pied Piper followers
40. Tranquilizer gun projectile
41. Gently shift to a new topic
43. "___ Time, Next Year"
45. Dell products
47. Peru's peaks
51. Pants parts
54. Boston ___ Orchestra
57. Gardner of film
58. Allot, with "out"
59. Painter's layer
60. Attorney's field
61. Hair removal brand
62. Places for rent: abbr.
63. Drive-___

DOWN

1. Walrus relative
2. Work at a keyboard
3. Bouncy
4. View again
5. What a guitar may be hooked up to
6. Thurman of "Pulp Fiction"
7. Actress Turner
8. Modern surgical tool
9. Lance of the bench
10. Greyhound stop: abbr.
11. "Pick a card, ___ card"
19. Retailer's goods: abbr.
21. School transportation
23. "Ali ___ and the Forty Thieves"
24. Horses' gaits
26. Festive party
27. Kuwaiti ruler
28. "Go away!"
29. Change for a twenty
30. Suffix with million or billion
31. Catch in a stocking
33. House in Spain

37. Barbara of "I Dream of Jeannie"
39. DVR button
42. Unexpected sports outcome
44. Sail supports
46. Pet lovers' org.
48. Painter of melting watches
49. "___ Almighty," 2007 film

50. Old sayings
51. Trio after "K"
52. Extra wide, on a shoebox
53. Former Telecom giant
55. Alley ___
56. Frisk, with "down"

Solution on Page 303

ACROSS

1. Chew the rag
4. Writing tablets
8. Radar signal
12. Degree held by many a CEO
13. Portentous sign
14. ___ Ness Monster
15. Boy king of ancient Egypt
16. Break in the action
17. Impressed
18. Defeat soundly
20. Fischer's forte
21. Frozen potato brand
23. "Stop it!"
26. The "E" in Einstein's formula
31. Imbeciles
34. Famous Hun
35. Like grams and liters
36. Hula ___
37. TV's "___ and Greg"
41. Smart-mouthed
45. Girl in a Beach Boys song
48. Snare
49. "Fargo" director
50. Make a pick
52. Legal rights grp.
53. Detest
54. Morning droplets
55. Every now and ___

56. Pretentiously showy
57. Big name in kitchen gadgets

DOWN

1. Clock-setting std.
2. Neighbor on
3. Relaxing soak
4. Of the Arctic or Antarctic
5. Make smile
6. New ___, India
7. NBC sketch show
8. Unexciting
9. Rob of "Masquerade"
10. Chills, as champagne
11. Advanced degs.
19. Spinning part
20. Quitter's word
22. Antidrug agcy.
23. Lower, as the lights
24. "___ to Billy Joe"
25. Louse-to-be
27. Patriot Allen
28. ___ de Janeiro
29. Mop & ___: cleaning brand
30. Jabber
32. Neat
33. PTA meeting place
38. Loud, as a crowd
39. Fictional Butler

Solution on page 403

Puzzle 16

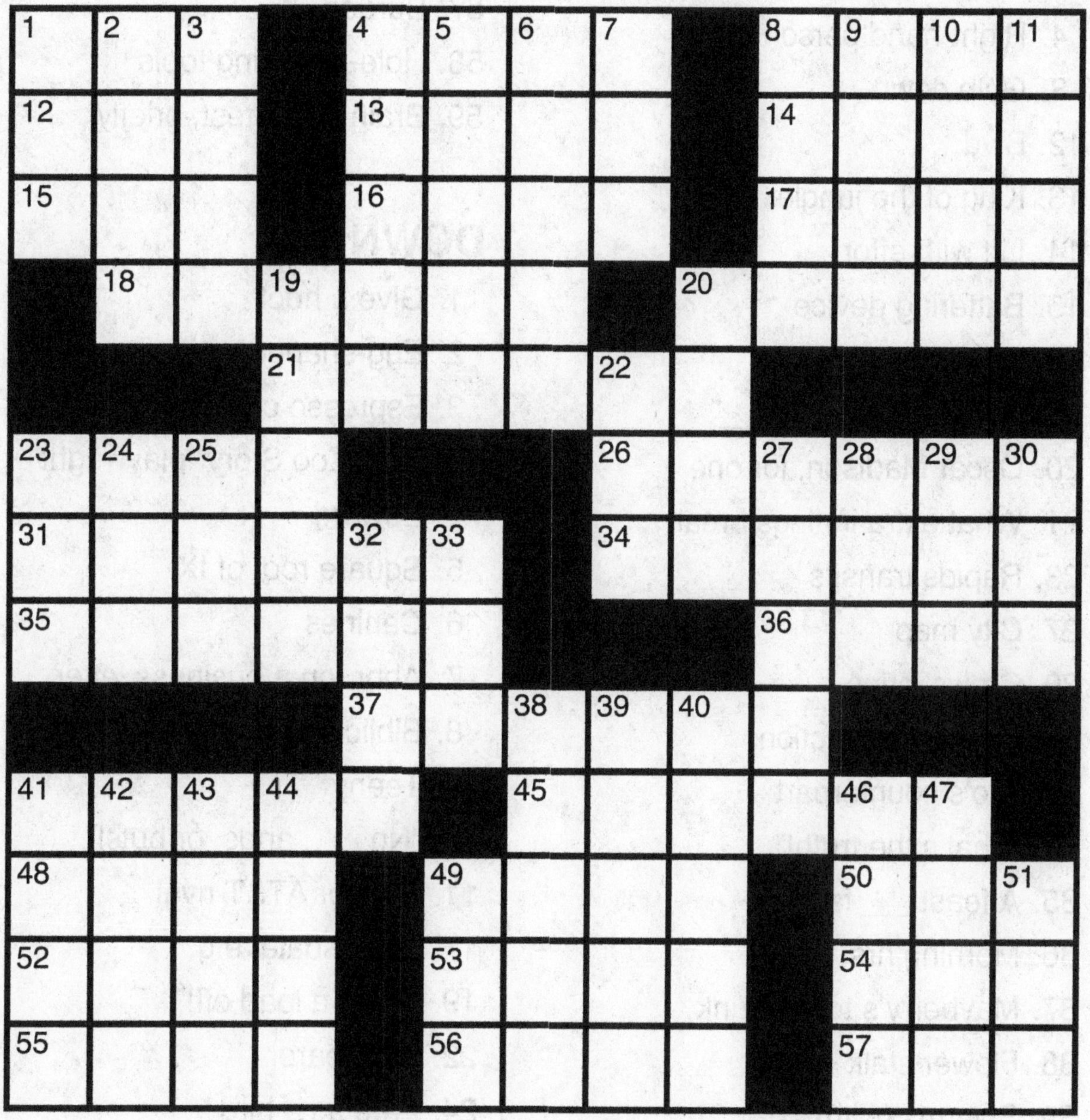

40. "Time is ___" (Benjamin Franklin aphorism)
41. Immediately, to a surgeon
42. Curved entranceway
43. Bargain hunter's delight
44. Whirled
46. Extinct flightless bird
47. Peak
49. "___-ching!" (cash register noise)
51. What it takes to tango

Solution on Page 303

ACROSS

1. New England fish
4. Right-hand person
8. Gulp down
12. Blvd.
13. King of the jungle
14. Lift with effort
15. Battering device
16. Head honcho
18. Beethoven's "Für ___"
20. Oscar Madison, for one
21. What extra innings break
23. Rapids transits
27. City map
29. Crows' cries
32. Fireworks reaction
33. Bro's counterpart
34. "That's the truth!"
35. A feast ___ famine
36. Morning hrs.
37. Mayberry's town drunk
38. Flower stalk
39. Swarms (with)
41. Transport, as a load
43. Prepares to fire
46. Cat chat
49. Spellbound
53. Salad dressing ingredient
54. "The ___ of Greenwich Village"
   (1984 movie)
55. '60s NASA target
56. Health club
57. Burden
58. Hole-punching tools
59. Brain-wave test, briefly

DOWN

1. Give a hoot
2. Egg-shaped
3. Espresso cup
4. "The Zoo Story" playwright
   Edward
5. Square root of IX
6. Canines
7. Abbr. on a business letter
8. Biblical land with a queen
9. Teeny
10. "No ___, ands, or buts!"
11. Former AT&T rival
17. Clydesdale, e.g.
19. "Take a load off!"
22. Kilt wearer
24. Free as a bird
25. Verbally attacked, with "into"
26. Sam the ___ and the Pharaohs
27. Exam for teens
28. Green shade
30. Outspoken boxer
31. Genie's offering
34. Military denial

38. Take to court

40. Spouses

42. Congregational cries

44. Papa's partner

45. Winter blanket

47. Use a dish towel

48. Smelting waste

49. NYSE debut

50. Negative prefix

51. "The Simpsons" storekeeper

52. Rank below general: abbr.

Solution on Page 304

ACROSS

1. Former veep Quayle
4. Flexible, electrically
8. Gulf War missile
12. Family card game
13. "Moonstruck" actress
14. Mexican coin
15. Insecticide banned since 1973
16. Saintly glow
17. Cheer (for)
18. Refrain in "Old MacDonald"
20. Michelle Wie's org.
22. Corn on the ___
24. Winona of "Girl, Interrupted"
28. Having a bit of smog
31. Prefix meaning "both"
34. Grammy winner Winehouse
35. News org. created in 1958
36. Noisy inhalation
37. Payable on demand
38. Youngster
39. Songstress Horne
40. Quarterback's option
41. Nutmeg, e.g.
43. LeBron James's org.
45. Had payments due
48. Peruvian beast
52. Lower leg
55. "G'day, ___!"
57. Sack
58. Hackman of Hollywood
59. Currier's partner
60. Tourney pass
61. Tongue-clicking sounds
62. Cincinnati baseball team
63. "Far out"

DOWN

1. Fellow, slangily
2. Me, myself, ___
3. Middle C, e.g.
4. Sound of a sneeze
5. When repeated, a Latin dance
6. Big name in computers
7. Field's yield
8. Aerosol output
9. Corp. head
10. Troop entertainment sponsor: abbr.
11. Period, in web addresses
19. Slippery, as winter sidewalks
21. Abrasive particles
23. Cause of one's undoing
25. Early baby word
26. Flightless flock
27. Deli breads
28. "Gilligan's Island" dwellings
29. Each, in pricing
30. Tubular pasta
32. "___ Dieu!"
33. Raisin ___ (cereal)

36. Dispatched, as a dragon

40. "Be a ___!"

42. Dairy Queen purchases

44. "God ___ America"

46. Kuwaiti chief

47. Brubeck of jazz

49. Shortened form, in shortened form

50. Poet Angelou

51. Got older

52. Friday's rank: abbr.

53. "___ a real nowhere man . . ."

54. Squid's squirt

56. Mack or Koppel

Solution on Page 304

ACROSS

1. I as in Innsbruck?
4. Baseball stats
8. What Eve was formed from
11. Unassertive
12. Determine weight by lifting
13. In ___ (coordinated)
14. Plenty ticked
15. "Piece of cake!"
16. Repair
17. Cub Scout groups
19. Olympic gymnast Korbut
21. Sept. preceder
23. Ahead of schedule
26. Jetsam's partner
30. Stiff-upper-lip type
32. Loo
33. 1996 candidate Dole
35. Dean's list fig.
36. Set straight
39. Holy
42. Improvise on stage
44. New Deal org.
45. Preteen's sch.
47. Beasts of burden
50. Lowly chess piece
53. Shredded
55. Hairstyling goop
57. In the near future
58. Have ___ (be connected)
59. Receive
60. I like ___
61. Wise man
62. Since 1/1, to a CPA

DOWN

1. Ideology
2. Punched-out part of a paper ballot
3. Half of a famous split personality
4. Medical research monkey
5. "Who Wants to ___ Millionaire?"
6. Should that be true . . .
7. Hair arrangement
8. Bread for a ham sandwich
9. A home away from home
10. Three before "E"
13. Like crossword solvers, naturally
18. ___ King Cole
20. Tank filler
22. Shoot the breeze
24. Fireplace fuel
25. "Holy cow!"
26. Miami's state: abbr.
27. Singsong syllables
28. Roman love poet
29. Rioting group
31. He's no gentleman
34. Diner sandwich
37. Actress Close
38. Not even one

40. Tennis champ Goolagong

41. Bill Clinton's instrument

43. Alphas' followers

46. Novelist Simpson

48. Like quiche or custard

49. Hair No More alternative

50. Letter before omega

51. Thumbs-up response

52. Misery

54. Fix, as a fight

56. Co. alternative

Solution on Page 304

ACROSS

1. Lose color
5. Up to the task
9. London's land: abbr.
12. Mountain ht.
13. Cowboy's footwear
14. Halen or Morrison
15. Round roof
16. "Ali ___ and the 40 Thieves"
17. Buy a pig ___ poke
18. Wasp weapon
20. Snow remover
21. Have a go at
22. Sot's spot
24. ___ and desist
27. Alcove near the kitchen
31. Olive ___ (Popeye's sweetie)
32. Build, as a monument
34. "To Each ___ Own"
35. 1970 Beatles chart-topper
37. At large
39. "___: Miami"
40. Fraternity members
41. "___, Where's My Car?" (2000 comedy)
44. Provide a voice-over
48. "___ quit!"
49. Camping stuff
51. Run ___ (go crazy)
52. "Leaving ___ Vegas"
53. Chooses (to)
54. Apportion, with "out"
55. Wapiti
56. Short race
57. Poke

DOWN

1. G-men
2. Plenty
3. Actress Moore
4. Occasions
5. Westminster ___
6. Part of an old English Christmas feast
7. High, arcing shot
8. Greek "H"
9. Wicked
10. iPod mini successor
11. Chew persistently
19. Says hello to
20. Post's opposite
22. Lighter and pen maker
23. Buck's defense
24. Newspaper div.
25. Hurricane's center
26. Height: abbr.
27. "Look at Me, I'm Sandra ___"
28. Ne'ertheless
29. "My Country, ___ of Thee . . ."
30. WNW's reverse

33. Baseball stat
36. Freezer trayful
38. Highway access
40. Wetland
41. Ration (out)
42. Russia's ___ Mountains
43. "Slipped" backbone part
44. Turner and Cole
45. Part of N.A.
46. Dog on the Yellow Brick Road
47. Managed, with "out"
49. In ___ We Trust
50. Clean Air Act org.

Solution on Page 304

ACROSS

1. Not Rep. or Dem.
4. Golfers' gadgets
8. Fem. opposite
12. "___ look like a mind reader?"
13. Freeway access
14. Prefix with lateral
15. Mantra syllables
16. ABA member: abbr.
17. Puny puppy
18. Withdraw (from)
20. Renter's paper
21. Give a new title to
24. Tennessee Senator Alexander
27. Holiday quaff
28. Packers' org.
31. Leaning
32. ___picker (overly critical one)
33. Unadulterated
34. On the ___ (furtively)
35. Bout enders, briefly
36. Golfer Palmer, familiarly
37. Opposed (to)
39. Beauty parlor
43. Be against
47. Big-screen format
48. Artist's inspiration
50. Free from, with "of"
51. It may be drawn in the sand
52. "The doctor ___"
53. Nest item
54. "Chestnuts roasting ___ open fire"
55. Tot's "piggies"
56. Hardly gregarious

DOWN

1. Nuptial exchanges
2. City on Seward Peninsula
3. A wink in a game of tiddlywinks, e.g.
4. ___ Vic's (restaurant chain)
5. Consumed
6. CPR specialist
7. Finder of secrets
8. "___ words cannot express . . ."
9. Shade of blue
10. Solar-system centers
11. Quote
19. Time periods
20. Relay race part
22. Licorice-like flavoring
23. Bon ___ (witticism)
24. There are 2.2 in a kg.
25. Feel poorly
26. Spring month
28. Convent dweller
29. Thurs. follower
30. Director Spike
32. Election mo.
33. Kind of school

35. Neb. neighbor

36. Colorado trees

38. TV host O'Donnell

39. Barn attachment

40. Idi of Uganda

41. "The Sweater Girl" Turner

42. Yoked beasts

44. Loads from lodes

45. Audible breath

46. Tense

48. "Good Will Hunting" school

49. Troop-entertaining grp.

Solution on Page 305

ACROSS

1. Cease
5. "___ the wind and nothing more"
8. Petty quarrel
12. ___ to one's word
13. Smart ___ whip
14. Carry
15. Combustible heap
16. Nurse a drink
17. "I cannot tell ___"
18. Profit's opposite
20. Leopard features
21. ___ up (paid)
24. Chat room guffaw
25. Fibbers
26. Web-footed mammals
29. Appropriate
30. Wet ground
31. Where Switz. is
33. Confidential matter
36. Arcade game maker
38. Play part
39. Pooped out
40. Barton of the Red Cross
43. Auctioneer's closing word
45. Ashen
46. ___ Zeppelin
47. Gross
51. No ifs, ___, or buts
52. Fort ___, Calif.
53. Buffalo's lake
54. Caribbean and Mediterranean
55. "___ it something I said?"
56. Rollick or frolic

DOWN

1. Engine additive brand
2. "Give it the old college ___"
3. Your and my
4. Spud preparer's tool
5. Soviet news service
6. Egyptian fertility goddess
7. Gullible person
8. Paper clip alternative
9. Game on horseback
10. Going ___ tooth and nail
11. Golf pegs
19. Takes too much of a drug
20. Drunkard
21. ___ carte
22. Playful bites
23. London's ___ Gallery
24. Inc., in England
26. Ump's call
27. Backside
28. Confident
30. "When Harry ___ Sally . . ."
32. Get ___ of (toss out)
34. Stroke gently
35. Major TV maker

36. The "A" in NATO: abbr.

37. Neater

40. Tax pros: abbr.

41. Penny ___ (1967 Beatles chart-topper)

42. Hawkeye portrayer

43. Word repeated after "Que" in a song

44. Bookie's quote

46. Daily temperature extreme

48. ___-Magnon

49. "Bette Davis Eyes" singer Carnes

50. Nope's opposite

Solution on Page 305

ACROSS

1. "My Gal ___"
4. "Just a ___!" ("Hold on!")
7. Bread unit
11. Uganda's ___ Amin
12. Toledo's lake
14. Humorist Bombeck
15. Actor Torn
16. "Cinderella" stepsister
18. Company with a spectacular 2001 bankruptcy
20. Letters on a phone's "0" button
21. PC "oops" key
22. Alamo offering
26. Norman Vincent ___
28. Fish feature
29. "Don't Bring Me Down" band, for short
30. Reverse, as an action
31. Wee one
32. Hit with the fist
33. Soapmaker's solution
34. Yahtzee cube
35. Agenda details
36. Mocking bird
38. Bite like a pup
39. Lubricates
41. Theater school study
44. Socially uncomfortable
48. Comic Conway

49. Entryway
50. "West ___ Story"
51. Med. plan
52. Aardvark's diet
53. Coffee-to-go topper
54. Affirmative

DOWN

1. Filly's father
2. Server's edge, in tennis
3. One who can see what you're saying
4. Hand-holding, spirit-raising get-together
5. White-tailed eagle
6. Italian farewell
7. Acquire knowledge
8. Surgery sites, briefly
9. "What ___, chopped liver?"
10. Gov't air-safety org.
13. ___ de corps
17. High schooler, probably
19. Norway's capital
23. Mind reading
24. Graduate, for short
25. Captains' records
26. Solid parts of orange juice
27. Irish folksinger
28. Friend's opposite
31. Bestseller list entries

32. Mix together

34. "That oughta ___!"

35. . . . need is a friend ___

37. Lion sounds

40. Compete in the America's Cup

42. Silent performer

43. Famous cookie maker

44. Where Boise is: abbr.

45. Chaney of old films

46. Parcel of land

47. "Star Wars" mil. project

Solution on Page 305

ACROSS

1. PC's "brain"
4. Real heel
7. Supplementary feature
12. Feel sick
13. "Roses ___ red . . ."
14. Ross of the Supremes
15. Bar code
16. Major TV brand
17. Rural's opposite
18. "I ___ to recall . . ."
20. Auto racer Yarborough
22. Proofreader's find
24. Away from home
25. EMT's forte
28. Rise from a chair
30. Singer/actress Zadora
31. Gets the soap off
34. Cell occupant
37. Environmentalist's prefix
38. Four: prefix
40. Greyhound vehicle
41. ___ one-eighty
42. Computer text can be written in this
46. Writing tools
47. Realtor's favorite sign
48. What a protractor measures
51. Untold centuries
54. .001 of an inch
55. Scrooge
56. ET's craft
57. Fannie ___
58. Shelter from the sun
59. Animal foot
60. Banners on the Internet

DOWN

1. Make happen
2. Peter the pepper picker
3. Painful stomach problem
4. Garage contents
5. ___ de Triomphe
6. Church official
7. No longer a minor
8. Dreadful
9. Apply, as ointment
10. Stop ___ dime
11. Bert Bobbsey's twin
19. It grows on trees
21. Taxpayer's dread
23. Numbered hwy.
25. Tax pro, for short
26. Peach center
27. "Norma ___"
29. ___ Martin (James Bond car)
31. Confederate soldier
32. Hospital area with many IVs
33. Dissenting votes
35. Pro-gun org.
36. Catholic ritual

39. Relent
41. Tractor maker John
43. Pause indicator
44. Homer epic
45. Sits in neutral
46. Answered a charge in court
48. Pro-___ (certain tourneys)

49. Biomedical research org.
50. Cookie-selling org.
52. Three ___ kind
53. At this moment

Solution on Page 305

ACROSS

1. Iron Maiden's "Hallowed Be ___ Name"
4. Dog food once hawked by Ed McMahon
8. Made, as a web
12. Tic-tac-toe victory
13. Fly high
14. "Where the heart is"
15. Mouse-spotter's cry
16. Medical breakthrough
17. Date with an MD
18. Ten: prefix
20. Finish, with "up"
22. Milky gem
25. Sonnets and such
29. Serving with chop suey
32. Cry of unveiling
34. Lennon's widow Yoko
35. Certain look-alike
38. "Alice" spin-off
39. Phone abbr.
40. Letter carriers' grp.
41. Boxer Mike
43. Connery of Bond films
45. "See ya"
47. Roseanne star
50. Do ___ others as . . .
53. Cinco de ___
56. Bumbler
58. Spy
59. Talking equine of TV
60. Caustic substance
61. Circle segments
62. Cry of surprise
63. "Acid"

DOWN

1. It may test the waters
2. Broke new ground?
3. Oxen connector
4. Songwriters' grp.
5. "Skip to My ___"
6. ___ for the course
7. City NNW of Provo
8. Mold
9. Rice Krispies sound
10. "Steee-rike!" caller
11. Tennis court divider
19. Joel or Ethan of film
21. Elliptical
23. Leave ___ (act gratuitously?)
24. Shoestrings
26. Columns' counterparts
27. Scissors cut
28. Awfully long time
29. Falling-out
30. Lazily
31. Corp. heads
33. Take risks

36. Crooner Bennett
37. Bluefin, for one
42. Double reeds
44. Dwelling
46. Television award
48. Food item served in a basket
49. They're soaked up at the beach

50. Thurman of "Kill Bill" films
51. ___'easter
52. That special touch, briefly
54. Magnate Onassis
55. Informal affirmative
57. Gave dinner

Solution on Page 306

ACROSS

1. Sternward
4. Swab
7. Gives in to gravity
11. Black-eyed ___
12. Book before Romans
14. "___, ma! No hands!"
15. Take the odds
16. Egg holder
17. Rooney of "60 Minutes"
18. Steam bath
20. Santa's helpers
22. It's north of Okla.
23. Fight (for)
24. " . . . golden days of ___"
27. Letter after wye
28. Place to play darts
31. ___ and feather
32. ___ fatty acid
34. The Monkees' "___ Believer"
35. ER workers
36. Medium size: abbr.
37. Without women
38. USO show audience
39. School support gp.
41. Beetle Bailey's boss
43. Stalin's predecessor
46. The Crimson Tide, familiarly
47. ___-do-well
49. KFC's Sanders, e.g.

51. Big name in chips
52. "Go, ___!"
53. AC stat
54. Three tsps.
55. USN officers
56. Ryan or Tilly

DOWN

1. Alert to squad cars, briefly
2. Service charges
3. "Toodle-oo"
4. Food from heaven
5. Atlantic or Pacific
6. Liquid meas.
7. Underground Railroad "passenger"
8. Absolutely the best
9. Deities
10. Shade of blue
13. Apple cofounder Jobs
19. Tiny Tim's instrument
21. Falsehoods
24. From Jan. 1 until now, in accounting
25. Dinghy propeller
26. $200 Monopoly properties: abbr.
27. Zig's opposite
28. "The ___ and the Pendulum"
29. Thurman of "The Avengers"
30. "Paper or plastic?" item
32. Calc prerequisite

1	2	3		4	5	6			7	8	9	10
11				12		13			14			
15				16					17			
	18		19				20	21				
		22				23						
24	25	26				27				28	29	30
31				32	33					34		
35				36					37			
			38				39	40				
	41	42					43			44	45	
46					47	48				49		50
51					52					53		
54						55				56		

33. Take offense at

37. ___ Antonio

38. Take hold of

39. Skirt fold

40. Contract provisions

41. Volvo rival

42. Vanderbilt and Grant

44. Long-range weapon, for short

45. Memo

46. Crunchy sandwich

48. Snaky swimmer

50. Schlep

Solution on Page 306

ACROSS

1. Mortgage org.
4. Call ___ day (retire)
7. Slender woodwind
11. Soup container
12. Partner of rank and serial number
14. Pepsi, e.g.
15. Popular TV police drama
16. "Sesame Street" skills
17. The "U" of CPU
18. Uses needle and thread
20. Eagle's claws
22. Stockholm resident
24. Mama's mate
25. New Jersey hoopsters
26. Reproduced word for word
29. Choose
30. Heredity units
31. Halloween cry
33. Apartment dwellers
35. Robe for Caesar
36. Kazan who directed "On the Waterfront"
37. Cut off
38. Fold, as paper
41. Stadium cover
42. Lion's den
43. Pinot ___ (wine)
45. "___ favor"
48. Clearasil target
49. Gait between walk and canter
50. Without further ___ . . .
51. Venison source
52. B&O and Reading
53. Stimpy's cartoon buddy

DOWN

1. Airwaves regulatory gp.
2. My dog ___ fleas
3. Licorice-flavored cordial
4. Thunderstruck
5. Keep ___ on (watch)
6. HBO competitor
7. Eye-related
8. U2 lead singer
9. Ken of "thirtysomething"
10. Sups
13. Monticello and Mount Vernon, e.g.
19. Koch and Asner
21. Gorillas
22. Start with Cone or Cat
23. Openly grieved
24. Ship of Columbus
26. Not strict
27. Better than average
28. Theater box
30. Guys' partners
32. Paddle

34. "___ My God to Thee"

35. Pro ___: for now

37. Arranges by type

38. Dressed (in)

39. Indy 500, e.g.

40. Mozart's "___ kleine Nachtmusik"

41. Christian in fashion

44. Bruin legend Bobby

46. Beethoven's "___ to Joy"

47. L. ___ Hubbard

Solution on Page 306

ACROSS

1. Over-50 grp.
5. "Hey, you!"
9. "A Nightmare on ___ Street"
12. "Guilty" or "not guilty"
13. Lead-in to "girl"
14. Compete
15. Flower holders
16. Monty Hall offering
17. Boise's state: abbr.
18. Turner and Danson
19. Mail Boxes ___
20. Dropped drug
21. ___ of Sandwich
24. Feeling blue
26. Groupie
29. More's opposite
31. Winnie-the-___
34. Stir up
36. One-celled protozoan
38. Pie pans
39. "The X-Files" agent Scully
41. Queue after "Q"
42. The U.S.'s "uncle"
44. Aspiring atty.'s exam
46. "Med" or "law" lead-in
48. Night school subj.
50. Epic tale
54. "A," in Austria
55. Business attire
57. Mountaintop
58. QB's scores
59. Part of USA
60. Seldom seen
61. Observe
62. Sammy with three 60-homer seasons
63. Snow glider

DOWN

1. Scheduled mtg.
2. Succulent houseplant
3. No longer working: abbr.
4. No longer fashionable
5. Writing tablet
6. Makes tough
7. Ballpark figure?
8. Bathroom powders
9. Villain
10. Tops
11. Lake formed by Hoover Dam
22. Capp and Capone
23. Hollow-stemmed plant
25. Military address: abbr.
26. Lard, essentially
27. Mr. Onassis
28. Hogwash
30. Without: French
32. Delivery room doctors, for short
33. Derby or bowler

35. The Beach Boys' "Surfin' ___"
37. Barnyard bleat
40. Axis foes
43. Flat-topped hills
45. Romanov rulers
46. Beloved animals
47. Hitcher's hope

49. Kind of wrestling
51. "C'mon, be ___!"
52. "Pretty Woman" star Richard
53. Abruptly dismissed
56. "La la" lead-in

Solution on Page 306

ACROSS

1. "Terrible" age
4. Healing formation
8. Fight for air
12. Eminem's genre
13. Housebroken
14. "___ Breaky Heart" (1992 hit)
15. Univ. e-mail ending
16. Paddy product
17. Salty drop
18. Boot camp affirmative
20. Join forces
21. Moon-landing program
24. Loosen, as a knot
27. Least difficult
32. Actor Sean
33. Princeton greenery
34. Naughty deed
35. Capital of New Mexico
37. ___ Park (Edison's lab site)
38. Calorie counter
40. Same for me
44. Baby's noisemaker
48. Frozen waffle brand
49. Heavy shoe
51. Jr.'s son
52. Cut of meat
53. Roof edge
54. Vehicle with sliding doors
55. Barks
56. Switchboard worker: abbr.
57. Meditation sounds

DOWN

1. Card with three pips
2. Walk through water
3. Musical work
4. Zebra feature
5. Egyptian capital
6. Onetime Jeep mfr.
7. Spelling competition
8. Fence opening
9. Taiwanese PC maker
10. Uneven hairdo
11. Flammable pile
19. Holy one
20. Cal. pages
22. Flood embankment
23. Deposit, as an egg
24. Raises, as the ante
25. Cultural grant giver, for short
26. "Grand Ole Opry" airer
28. Motionless
29. An eternity
30. Lorne Michaels show, for short
31. "Not a moment ___ soon!"
33. "___ were you . . ."
36. Noisy commotion
37. Scanty
39. "Treasure ___"

40. Creme ___ creme
41. Composer Stravinsky
42. End-of-week cry
43. Heaps
45. Save for later viewing
46. Author O'Flaherty
47. ___, zwei, drei

49. Business VIP
50. Runner's circuit

Solution on Page 307

ACROSS

1. Spoiled kid
5. Famous Uncle
8. Declared
12. Beer choice
13. Nonwinning tic-tac-toe line
14. Peruvian capital
15. "Uncle ___ Cabin"
16. Actor Beatty
17. In ___: stuck
18. Label
20. Big Board letters
21. Cutting rays
24. Captain's journal
26. Battery terminal
27. "You've ___ Mail"
28. Up, up, and away defunct flier
31. Gives a thumbs-up
32. Raise a glass to
34. Jury-___ (improvise)
35. ___ Paulo, Brazil
36. "Wise" bird
37. Make amends
39. Hollywood's Howard
40. Stockholm natives
41. Post-it, e.g.
44. Palindromic Bobbsey twin
45. Big rabbit features
46. Fish-to-be
48. Trucker's rig

52. "This ride is great!"
53. Pub drink
54. McGregor of "Angels & Demons"
55. Bird-feeder block
56. The "p" in mpg
57. Gardener's bagful

DOWN

1. Sandwich letters
2. Brazilian vacation spot, informally
3. $20 bill dispenser
4. Tried out
5. Musical numbers
6. Tree feller
7. "The ___ Squad" of '60s–'70s TV
8. Informal language
9. Breezy
10. Don of talk radio
11. Palm fruit
19. "Am not!" rejoinder
21. Neighbor of Cambodia
22. "Puppy Love" singer Paul
23. Just okay
24. Part of L.A.
25. Canada's capital
27. Lass
28. Walked all over
29. Chianti or chablis
30. "Rock of ___"
33. Have title to

[crossword grid]

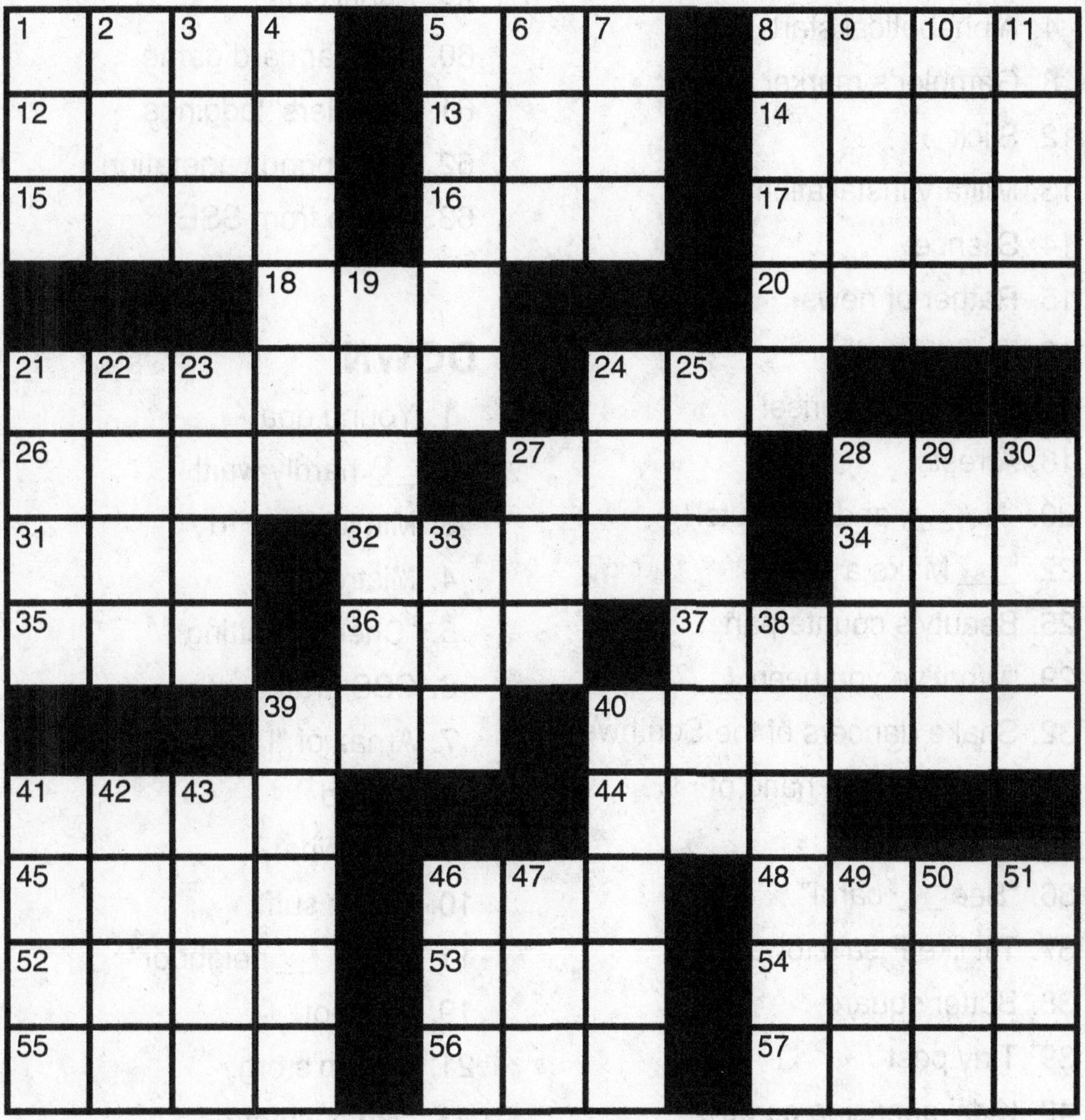

38. Past, present, and future

39. Put back to 000

40. Look of disdain

41. Part of CNN

42. Home to Honolulu

43. Apple or maple

46. Jay-Z's music genre

47. Cheer for a bullfighter

49. She sheep

50. Fannie ___ (federal mortgage agency)

51. Like Perot's party: abbr.

Solution on Page 307

ACROSS

1. Basinger of "Batman"
4. Alphabetical start
8. Gambler's marker
12. Slick
13. Military installation
14. Silence
15. Rather of news
16. "Trinity" author
17. "That's a surprise!"
18. Arrests
20. "No ___, ands, or buts!"
22. "___ Make a Deal"
25. Beauty's counterpart
29. "What've you been ___?"
32. Snake dancers of the Southwest
34. Try to win the hand of
35. Chair or sofa
36. "See ___ care!"
37. Tilt like Pisa's tower
38. Butter square
39. Tiny pest
40. Kids' guessing game
41. Coil of yarn
43. Hot Japanese drink
45. Soup order
47. Get rid of
50. Word processor's "cancel that last step"
53. The Bruins of the NCAA
56. Use an ax
58. Popular lunch hour
59. Badly claw
60. Popular card game
61. Travelers' lodgings
62. Bit of pond vegetation
63. U-turn from SSE

DOWN

1. Young goat
2. ___ hardly wait!
3. Mimicking bird
4. Mistreat
5. "Cheers" setting
6. CBS drama
7. Arnaz of "I Love Lucy"
8. Picked
9. "Say what?"
10. Belief: suff.
11. "Love ___ neighbor"
19. Ink spot
21. G-man's org.
23. Like a wafer
24. Couches
26. Amazes
27. Cleansing agent
28. Cereal spokestiger
29. Letter carriers' org.
30. Pinnacle
31. London art gallery
33. Bread for a gyro

72

37. In ___ of (replacing)

39. Bearded grassland dweller

42. Computer symbols

44. Furry marsupial

46. Mountain lion

48. Stay away from

49. State south of Ky.

50. Bi- halved

51. ___ sequitur

52. Ho of Hawaii

54. Ripken of the diamond

55. Carry with difficulty

57. "I'm impressed!"

Solution on Page 307

ACROSS

1. Blubber
4. Workout centers
8. Tanning lotion letters
11. Gave a thumbs-up
13. The ___ McCoy
14. Mincemeat dessert
15. ___ jail (Monopoly directive)
16. Get ___ shape
17. ___ and downs
18. Inc. alternative
20. Fairy tale monsters
22. "Say cheese!"
25. Knocks lightly
27. ___ Cruces, New Mexico
28. Top spot
30. Points at the target
34. Israeli weapon
35. 12" stick
37. "Uh-uh"
38. List of choices
40. Zilch
41. Feed lines to
42. Hellish river
44. Hiker's path
46. "___ Doesn't Live Here Anymore"
49. "The Partridge Family" actress Susan
50. Karaoke singer's need, for short
51. Naked
54. St. Louis's Gateway ___
58. Leap day's mo.
59. Sketched
60. Yep's opposite
61. "The word," to secret keepers
62. Knock 'em dead
63. Dryly humorous

DOWN

1. Part of a gearwheel
2. "Top Hat" studio
3. "Are we there ___?"
4. Graph paper pattern
5. Tokyo money
6. Wrestling surface
7. Single-masted boat
8. Thing on a cowboy's boot
9. Popeye's tooter
10. ___ up (come clean)
12. Raggedy Ann, e.g.
19. Drop from the eye
21. Cookie-selling gp.
22. Squalid neighborhood
23. Lab rat's challenge
24. Beauty ___ the eye . . .
25. "Stop worrying!"
26. Chopped down
29. Measly
31. Ancient Peruvian
32. Hawaii's "Valley Isle"
33. Writer/illustrator Silverstein

36. Evaluate

39. O. J.'s alma mater

43. Minds, as a bar

45. Actress Meg

46. Radio switch

47. In ___ of (instead of)

48. Warhead weapon, for short

49. Moist, as morning grass

52. Web address, for short

53. Narcs' org.

55. Propel a dinghy

56. EMS procedure

57. "___ Jude" (Beatles classic)

Solution on Page 307

ACROSS

1. El ___ (Heston role)
4. On pins and needles
8. Prominent Durante feature
12. Single: prefix
13. Hawaiian cookout
14. Heroic tale
15. Cable modem alternative, briefly
16. Lounge around
17. Presidential rejection
18. Sight organ
20. Lagasse of the Food Network
22. "Friends, ___, countrymen"
25. Native of Tehran
26. Military force
27. Grasp
30. Corporate bigwig's deg.
31. Roswell sighting
32. Computer key
35. Facts
36. Auto brand
37. Disney World's ___ Center
41. Throat extract, at times
43. Not wide
45. Bon ___ (clever remark)
46. ___ laughing (cracks up)
47. Bees' home
50. "Yikes!"
53. "Render ___ Caesar . . ."
54. Words of confidence
55. Slugger's stat
56. Ball-___ hammer
57. Shea team
58. Hoops grp.

DOWN

1. What a cow chews
2. ___ and outs
3. Perplexing problem
4. Comic DeGeneres
5. Simon & Garfunkel, once
6. Guy's partner
7. Christmas season
8. "And ___ the twain shall meet"
9. Met offering
10. Peaceful protest
11. Food-poisoning bacteria
19. Palindromic cheer
21. Prefix with life or wife
22. Ewe's mate
23. Sun or moon, to bards
24. Avoid deliberately
28. "They're ___!" (racetrack cry)
29. Ill-gotten goods
32. Part of EDT
33. Slide down a slope
34. "Fantasia" frame
35. "Am ___ blame?"
36. "L–P" filler
37. This ___ (shipping label)

38. Revolutionary pamphleteer Thomas

39. Largest Greek island

40. Welles or Bean

42. Signs of things to come

44. Sudden impulse

48. Swelling reducer

49. Large container

51. Decline

52. Sedona maker

Solution on Page 308

ACROSS

1. Dunce cap, geometrically
5. Seek office
8. It follows April in Paris
11. Throat clearer
12. King Kong, e.g.
13. Good for what ___ you
14. Drove like mad
15. Oft-stubbed digit
16. 1982 sci-fi film
17. Pleasantly brief
20. Obtain
21. ___ Na Na
22. Weapons stash
26. "Fear of Fifty" writer Jong
30. "___ and Me Against the World"
31. "___ Legit to Quit"
33. Partners of don'ts
34. Hot coal
37. Manet and Monet
40. Opp. of ant.
42. Charged particle
43. Unwanted possession
50. Conceal
51. Ballpoint, e.g.
52. Song for a diva
53. ___ about (approximately)
54. Fore's opposite
55. Yearn (for)
56. City in GA
57. Some USN officers
58. Rams' mates

DOWN

1. Tabbies
2. "Oops!"
3. Infamous Roman emperor
4. Come out
5. Tommy gun noise
6. "Once ___ a midnight dreary . . ."
7. Necessary things
8. Oozy ground
9. Lotion ingredient
10. "Money ___ everything!"
13. In armed conflict
18. Commandments count
19. "That's all ___ wrote"
22. Affirmative at sea
23. CD-___ (computer insert)
24. Classroom replacement
25. Mauna ___ (brand of macadamia nuts)
27. Proof-of-age items, for short
28. Army bed
29. Donkey's cousin
32. Familiarizes with new surroundings
35. Fragrant compound
36. Ham on ___
38. Outdo

39. Fill the lungs

41. Kathmandu's land

43. "Hold it right there!"

44. Help for the stumped

45. False god

46. Not right

47. "And pretty maids all in ___"

48. Cloud number

49. Labels

Solution on Page 308

ACROSS

1. Construction site watchdog, for short
5. Heap praise on
9. PC core
12. Sword fight, e.g.
13. Twisted
14. Buffoon
15. Give out cards
16. Answering-machine sound
17. Batman and Robin, e.g.
18. German dessert
20. Snakelike fish
21. Harrison or Reed
22. Comic book punch sound
24. Uses as a reference
27. Like some traits
31. "This ___ fine how-do-you-do!"
32. Online letter
34. Small bite
35. Clothing
37. Part of ancient Asia Minor
39. Mo. Metropolis
40. Bus. name ending
41. Woman's undergarment
44. Dangerous African flies
48. Postpone, with "off"
49. Motel amenity
51. Tulsa's state: abbr.
52. Little ___ (tots)
53. Bigger than big
54. Animal hide
55. Bit of sunlight
56. Darn!
57. "___ only trying to help"

DOWN

1. Chances
2. Fatty treat for birds
3. "Now ___ this!"
4. Magnetism
5. Material for a doctor's glove
6. Illegally off base
7. Ornamental vase
8. Color changer
9. Morse's creation
10. Legendary Bunyan
11. Roswell sightings
19. Gobi or Mojave
20. Ram's mate
22. Architect I. M. ___
23. Connected to the Internet
24. Espionage org.
25. EarthLink, e.g.
26. Spigot
27. "My ___ Sal"
28. Old cable inits.
29. Three on a sundial
30. Number cruncher, for short
33. Singer Tillis

36. Deadly snake

38. Eight-armed creatures

40. Speck in the sea

41. Cowboy boot attachment

42. Moon goddess

43. Teeny, informally

44. Roman robe

45. Slant unfairly

46. Jazzy Fitzgerald

47. Pre-coll. exams

49. Advanced degree: abbr.

50. Lord's Prayer start

Solution on Page 308

ACROSS

1. Carry-___ (small pieces of luggage)
4. Cable TV's "C-___"
8. Religious faction
12. Enemy
13. Radial, e.g.
14. "Up, Up, and ___"
15. Former Pan Am rival
16. "Look ___ when I'm talking to you!"
17. Ky. neighbor
18. Chip dip
20. Hindu social division
21. Perfectly timed
23. University VIP
25. Fans' sound
26. Volcanic flow
27. Mtge. units
30. Texas border town
32. ___ Doria (ill-fated ship)
34. One of the Three Stooges
35. Aloha gifts
37. January to December
38. Makes clothes
39. Croatian-born physicist Nikola
40. Performed on stage
43. Elevate
45. Naughty child's Christmas gift
46. Enclosure with a MS.
47. Hoopsters' org.
50. "Ready or not, here I ___!"
51. Estate receiver
52. Indent key
53. Recipe measures: abbr.
54. 'Tis a shame
55. Kangaroo pouch

DOWN

1. Frequently, in verse
2. At once
3. Shore scene
4. No longer fresh
5. Peach centers
6. Fleet of warships
7. Maiden name preceder
8. The Prince of Darkness
9. She sheep
10. "Sheesh, ___ you read?"
11. Daly of "Judging Amy"
19. Luminous radiation
20. James of TV's "Las Vegas"
21. Fast-growing city near Provo
22. Court plea, for short
24. Gabor and Peron
26. Big name in movie theaters
27. Gifts
28. Bluish green
29. ___ Lee cakes
31. Iditarod vehicle
33. Henna and others

36. Tel Aviv's land
38. Tennis great Monica
39. Stadium levels
40. The "A" of IRA: abbr.
41. Dove, or love, murmurs
42. Press down, as pipe tobacco
44. Where the Himalayas are

46. ___ Na Na
48. Sheep's sound
49. Alphabetical network

Solution on Page 308

ACROSS

1. Grade between bee and dee
4. Soak up, as gravy
7. Splinter group
11. "I dropped it!"
13. Linden of "Barney Miller"
14. iPod type
15. Make a sweater
16. Approx. landing hour
17. ___ cost (free)
18. Break out of jail
20. Bit of advice
22. Like the season before Easter
24. Get handed a bum ___
27. Like Pisa's tower
30. Acorn's source
31. Former Roxy Music member Brian
32. Agrees nonverbally
33. "R" followers
34. Trash holders
35. Scheduled to arrive
36. Honey maker
37. Not true
38. A Gershwin brother
39. Egg hunt holiday
41. Taxi
42. San Simeon castle-builder
46. Lose brilliance
49. "Much ___ About Nothing"
51. Tortilla sandwich
52. Missing from the Marines, say
53. Madam's counterpart
54. Nose-in-the-air type
55. Pub offerings
56. Nine-digit ID
57. A Verizon predecessor

DOWN

1. Pepsi competitor
2. Many millennia
3. "Ben-Hur," for one
4. Luster
5. Bit of grain
6. Flat part of a chart line
7. Crackle and pop's partner
8. Chow down
9. Larry King's channel
10. "___ many cooks spoil the broth"
12. Plays for time
19. Classroom favorite
21. Calligrapher's liquid
23. Carries
24. Not imaginary
25. Landers and Sothern
26. Sit for a photo
27. "___ Love Her"
28. Military stint
29. Clever thought
33. "Chilean" fish
34. Gem units

84

36. "Don't ___ stranger"
37. Lawyer's charge
40. Pricker
41. Animation art pieces
43. Summoned Jeeves
44. Get off ___ free
45. Choice for Hamlet

46. Air safety agcy.
47. Piercing tool
48. Bambi's mother, for one
50. Insult, slangily

Solution on Page 309

ACROSS

1. Actress ___ Dawn Chong
4. Chow mein additive
7. Uses a sofa
11. "If looks could kill" type of stare
12. "Woe is me!"
14. Prefix with distant or lateral
15. Test for PhD wannabes
16. Likely legal precedents
18. Tranquilize
20. Popular cooking spray
21. Race, as an engine
22. Saudi ___
26. Strive
29. Renter
30. ___ constrictor
31. Comedian DeLuise
32. Not fine-grained
36. Cling (to)
39. Leisurely walk
40. Pasture
41. "Peggy ___ Got Married"
42. Frozen spear
46. Big crop in Hawaii
50. Lenient
51. Finish for teen or golden
52. "And ___ what happened?"
53. "Hail, Caesar!"
54. "Goodness!"
55. Fast jet, for short
56. Isn't anymore

DOWN

1. Fixes illegally
2. Farm unit
3. Ogled
4. Space occupier
5. Magician's hiding place
6. Neon or freon
7. Sailor
8. Mensa members have high ones
9. Early d. of the wk.
10. ___ boom bah
13. March 17 honoree, for short
17. Have concern
19. Onassis nickname
23. Expressed, as farewell
24. "Are you ___ out?"
25. "Don't look ___ like that!"
26. Kindergarten learning
27. Chimney grime
28. Carson's predecessor
33. Prayer beads
34. Speak unclearly
35. Vote into office
36. Flared skirts
37. Not half bad

38. "Bali ___" ("South Pacific" song)

43. Cat's scratcher

44. Volcanic overflow

45. Old flames

46. ___ Tome and Principe

47. "Gross!"

48. Ring rock

49. Sighs of contentment

Solution on Page 309

ACROSS

1. Noun modifier: abbr.
4. Corn bread
8. Griffin who created "Jeopardy!"
12. "La-la" lead-in
13. Get one's ducks in ___
14. In re
15. "A ___ for All Seasons"
16. Sup
17. Meal in a pot
18. Say four-letter words
20. Norwegian capital
22. Handful
24. Feeling of anxiety
28. Filmed
31. Some PCs
34. Thumbs-up vote
35. Break, as a balloon
36. Nabisco cookies
37. Glove compartment item
38. Australian bird
39. Vegas numbers game
40. Distinctive doctrines
41. Actor Romero
43. Detective Spade
45. Wrestling surfaces
48. Supply food for a fee
52. Actress Rogers who was once married to Tom Cruise
55. Fuzzy image
57. Palindromic Gardner
58. PC programs
59. Mailing courtesy: abbr.
60. ___ tai (drink)
61. ___ and aahs
62. School orgs.
63. Wrap up

DOWN

1. Cash dispensers, for short
2. Take a card
3. Author Austen
4. Mission priest
5. "Either he goes, ___ do!"
6. "___, Nanette"
7. Lambs' mothers
8. Bricklayer
9. Superlative suffix
10. P.O. worker's circuit
11. Solemn promise
19. Back, on a ship
21. Lad's mate
23. Word with hay or live
25. Workout sites
26. Stitched line
27. Bugler's evening call
28. Design detail
29. Where the heart is, they say
30. Numbered musical work
32. Oscar winner Kingsley
33. Cattle calls

1	2	3	■	4	5	6	7	■	8	9	10	11
12			■	13				■	14			
15			■	16				■	17			
18			19		■	20		21		■	■	■
■	■	22		23	■	■	24		■	25	26	27
28	29	30		■	31	32	33		■	34		
35			■	36				■	■	37		
38			■	39				■	40			
41			42		■	■	43	44		■	■	■
■	■	45		46	47	■	48		■	49	50	51
52	53	54		■	55		56		■	57		
58				■	59				■	60		
61				■	62				■	63		

36. Cajun veggie

40. John Denver's "Thank God ___ Country Boy"

42. Out of kilter

44. Land measures

46. Recipe amt.

47. Wood strip used as a bed support

49. Change from wild to mild

50. Writer Hunter

51. Surprise attack

52. ___ Tse-tung

53. Stock mkt. debut

54. Dashboard: abbr.

56. Springsteen's "Born in the ___"

Solution on Page 309

ACROSS

1. Big galoot
4. Peter the Great, for one
8. Family member
11. Shape of the president's office
13. Margarita fruit
14. Thing to play with
15. Land of Lima and llamas
16. Computer programs, for short
17. Fill with wonder
18. Inviting smell
20. Smidgens
22. Pisa landmark
24. Rumba or samba
26. End ___ high note
27. Nectar collectors
29. Bikini parts
32. Poehler of "Parks and Recreation"
33. Caught some Zs
35. Blubber
36. Scissorhands portrayer Johnny
38. Store inventory: abbr.
39. Capote's nickname
40. Cowboy's rope
42. Pale-faced
44. Ex-Mrs. Trump
46. Stan's slapstick partner
48. Christmas mo.
49. Nothin'
51. Places for experiments
54. Appomattox surrenderer
55. Melt
56. Ray who created the McDonald's empire
57. Decade divs.
58. Oohs' companions
59. Light opening?

DOWN

1. Alley ___
2. Street map abbr.
3. Exotic destinations
4. Chowder ingredient
5. "Song of the South" song
6. Sound booster
7. Pine exudation
8. Technologically advanced
9. Presidential caucus state
10. Farewells
12. Tackle box item
19. Globes
21. Tenth mo.
22. Warty hopper
23. Elton John's "Don't Let the Sun Go Down ___"
25. Vile Nile creatures
28. O'Neill's "Desire Under the ___"
30. Peel, as an apple

31. Shock

34. Greenish blue

37. Pie holder

41. Christmas visitor

43. Fine pajama material

44. Without purpose

45. Go off in a new direction

47. Cops enforce them

50. "So that's it!"

52. Arrow shooter

53. Biol. or chem.

Solution on Page 309

ACROSS

1. Jar tops
5. Color of embarrassment
8. Ernie or Gomer
12. On
13. Debunked mentalist Geller
14. Smell strongly
15. Rob of "St. Elmo's Fire"
16. In direct confrontation
18. "___ of Green Gables"
19. High-speed connection, for short
20. Florida's Miami-___ County
23. Lacking refinement
28. Lodge member
31. Miniature plateau
33. Worker protection org.
34. Net defender
36. Skin soother
38. "Going, going, ___!"
39. Bear with cold porridge
41. Basic version: abbr.
42. Dictation taker
44. Do a fall chore
46. Baseball hitting stat
48. ___-Israeli relations
52. Lessen
57. A fisherman may spin one
58. Suit to ___
59. Tyrannosaurus ___
60. Flulike symptoms
61. Formal dance
62. 180 degrees from WNW
63. Office worker just for the day

DOWN

1. In ___ land (daydreaming)
2. Have ___ good authority
3. Pillow filler
4. Drive too fast
5. It's boring to be in one
6. Eats away
7. Fizzles (out)
8. In favor of
9. "You ain't seen nothin' ___!"
10. Novelist Tolstoy
11. Earn laboriously, with "out"
17. Pampering, for short
21. Pal in Paris
22. Pass judgment
24. Decay
25. Without warranties
26. Gun blast
27. Beach composition
28. Breakfast order
29. Plunder
30. Citizen of film
32. ___ mater
35. Actor Cariou
37. "Mighty" fine home for a squirrel?
40. Comes up in conversation

43. Smelter input
45. Bother persistently
47. Unadorned
49. Extreme anger
50. Homecoming attender
51. Pager's sound
52. Mini-glob

53. Incoming flight info.
54. Animation unit
55. Seminary subj.
56. Palindromic English river

Solution on Page 310

ACROSS

1. "___ Doubtfire"
4. The Almighty
7. Playtex products
11. Spreadsheet lines
13. Breakfasted, e.g.
14. Agitate
15. Radiate
16. Compaq products
17. Archaeologist Jones, for short
18. Reduce in rank
20. Director's cry
22. "Children of a ___ God"
24. Major leaguer
27. Oregon capital
30. Prefix meaning "one"
31. Light knock
32. Stratford-upon-___
33. Battleship score
34. Minnelli of "Cabaret"
35. Spy org.
36. "Slippery when ___"
37. Caravan creature
38. Tax form ID
39. "We ___ amused"
41. Steady as ___ goes
42. Film cutter
46. Berlin Mrs.
49. Disabled vehicle's need
51. Half of Mork's signoff

52. "___ Gun Will Travel"
53. Anger
54. Miners' finds
55. Discoverers' cries
56. Ford or Lincoln
57. Ore. clock setting

DOWN

1. TV talking horse
2. Italy's capital
3. Sink's alternative
4. Stares open-mouthed
5. How some stocks are sold: abbr.
6. Mountain climber's return
7. Londoner, e.g.
8. "Apollo 13" director Howard
9. Assistance
10. Leader of the Family Stone
12. Like some kisses and bases
19. Chairman pro ___
21. Geller with a psychic act
23. High-end hotel option
24. ___ and proper
25. Completely demolish
26. October birthstone
27. Small pouches
28. Budget competitor
29. Bank offer
33. Religious dissenter
34. Mexican-American, e.g.

94

36. "Do ___ Diddy Diddy": 1964 song

37. Atlantic food fish

40. More recent

41. Litigates

43. Waterproof cover

44. Singles

45. What stainless steel doesn't do

46. D.C. mortgage insurer

47. Cheer

48. Gardner of Hollywood

50. A feast ___ famine

Solution on Page 310

ACROSS

1. ER drug disasters
4. Braying beast
7. Boutique
11. Goes bad
13. Blasting stuff
14. Prefix with -nautics
15. Put in the mail
16. Cow sound
17. Fishing line winder
18. Torch's crime
20. Many are about nothing
21. Proverbial waste-maker
24. Ball-shaped hammer part
26. Great grade
27. Taxpayer's ID
28. ___ baby makes three
31. Employ again
32. Tippy craft
34. Food additive
35. The "A" in ETA: abbr.
38. Jazz great Shaw
39. To ___: perfectly
40. Crystal ball users
41. Condo units: abbr.
44. Tim of "Home Improvement"
46. Man with an ark
47. Amorous murmur
48. Quickly!, on an order
52. Schnozzola
53. Catch some rays
54. College entrance exams
55. Clumsy boats
56. Star Wars program, for short
57. Foldaway bed

DOWN

1. Sterile hosp. areas
2. Anonymous John
3. Bus term.
4. After-hours money sources, for short
5. Nosy people
6. Jagger and the gang
7. Brand of wrap
8. Obey
9. Creme cookie
10. Campaign pros
12. ___ quo
19. Usher again
21. Cause damage to
22. "Planet of the ___"
23. Fake coin
25. Sheathe
28. Poker payment
29. Film ___ (movie genre)
30. "Disco Duck" singer Rick
33. Stadiums
36. Responds
37. Put in more ammo

39. Fireplace remnants

41. "___ and the King of Siam"

42. Like Franklin's Richard

43. Job to do

45. Burt's ex

49. Cul-de-___

50. From ___ Z (completely): 2 wds.

51. Winter clock setting in S.F.

Solution on Page 310

ACROSS

1. Do sums
4. "The Sun ___ Rises"
8. California wine county
12. Floral welcome
13. Sax vibrator
14. Actor Baldwin
15. Decreased
17. Minor quarrel
18. Cole and Turner
19. Abstains from eating
20. Truck stop stoppers
23. Kiss and ___
25. Like deserts
26. Gondola propeller
27. "___ Goes the Weasel"
30. Movie theater
32. Activity with chops and kicks
34. Chem. or phys.
35. Slant
37. Signal, as a cab
38. "No ___, no foul"
39. Samuel with a code
40. Gathers leaves
43. "Yikes!"
45. Prefix with bus or potent
46. Hawkeye Pierce portrayer
50. Vigoda and Lincoln
51. ___ and shine
52. Pro's opposite
53. Go easy on the calories
54. Bottle tops
55. Understand, in hippie lingo

DOWN

1. ___ or nothing
2. Poor mark
3. Speak ill of, in slang
4. Regions
5. Gave temporarily
6. Takes care of
7. Out of the ordinary
8. ___ congestion
9. Austrian peaks
10. ___ moss
11. "___ of the Apostles"
16. Nasty, as a remark
19. Kind of market or circus
20. Anatomical pouches
21. Idle of Monty Python
22. Above-the-knee skirt
24. Lodge members
26. Duo
27. Early late-night host
28. Elevator pioneer
29. Brazilian soccer legend
31. Degrees held by many CEOs
33. "The Mary Tyler Moore Show" spinoff
36. Aviator Earhart

38. Bank robber's job
39. Lions' locks
40. Highway
41. Prefix with dextrous
42. Deep ___ bend
44. Struggle for air
46. Pop fly's path

47. PC screen type
48. "Where ___ sign?"
49. "Brokeback Mountain" director Lee

Solution on Page 310

ACROSS

1. "No ___ luck!"
5. Hot dog holder
8. When said three times, a 1970 war film
12. "That ___ excuse"
13. ___ Wednesday
14. Popeye's greeting
15. Orange-flavored instant drink
16. Fam. reunion attendee
17. Lo-cal.
18. Column next to the ones
20. Sounds of amazement
21. Choo-choos
24. "___ voyage!"
26. Edmonton hockey player
27. Diarist Anaïs
28. .001 inch
31. Bon ___ (witty saying)
32. Draw ___ in the sand
34. Critical hosp. area
35. RR stop
36. Popular clothing store, with "The"
37. More grim
39. Chair part
40. Pay no mind to
41. Cartoon skunk Le Pew
44. Start of an invention
45. Greenish blue
46. ___-Magnon (early human)

47. Blueprint detail
51. Go left or right
52. Chum
53. Jazz's Fitzgerald
54. Knighted ones
55. Young' ___ (tots)
56. Hair untangler

DOWN

1. Command for Fido
2. Land north of Mex.
3. "Headline News" channel
4. Immobilize, rodeo-style
5. Buildings with lofts
6. Puts to work
7. Gretzky's org.
8. Eagle's claw
9. Home of the Buckeyes
10. Rocker David Lee ___
11. Affirmative votes
19. Infuriate
21. "Uncle ___ Cabin"
22. Unruly event
23. ___ Loma, Calif.
24. Storage container
25. Jittery
27. ___ and tuck
28. Spanish surrealist Joan
29. Cake decorator
30. Come-on

Puzzle 45

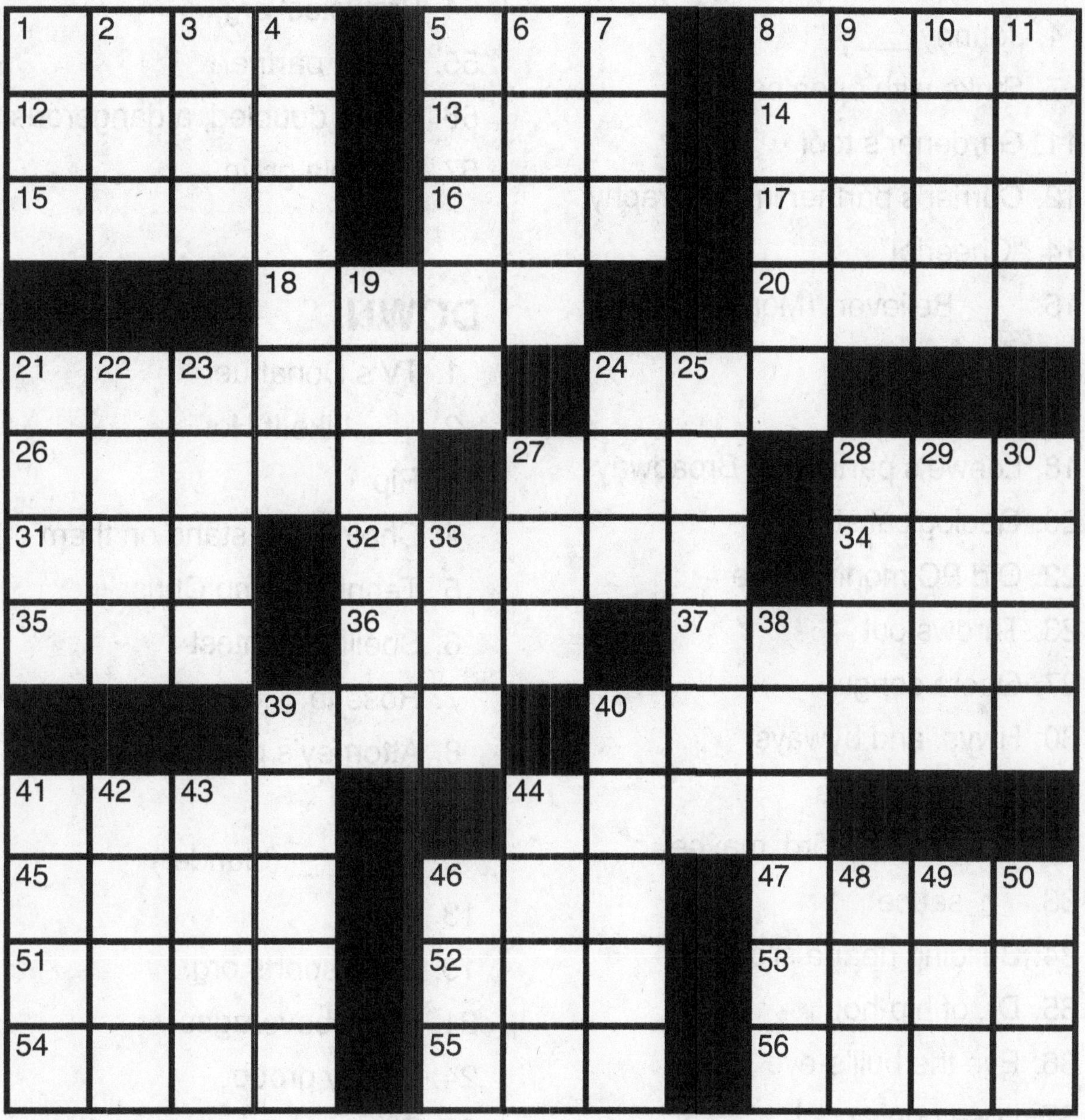

33. Word after jet or time
38. "I'll be right there!"
39. Tilts
40. Golden calf, et al.
41. Butter squares
42. Prefix meaning "same"
43. Sound of contentment
44. Tehran's land
46. Intel product, briefly
48. Arafat's group: abbr.
49. Stately tree
50. Urban ride

Solution on Page 311

ACROSS

1. Attention getter
4. Johnny ___
7. Strike with open hand
11. Gardener's tool
12. Currier's partner in lithography
14. "Cheerio!"
15. "___ Believer" (Monkees tune)
16. Ooze
17. Has a tab
18. Loewe's partner on Broadway
20. Geological stretch
22. Old PC monitor type
23. Throws out
27. Opera songs
30. Hwys. and byways
31. Actress Myrna
32. Baby's first word, maybe
33. ___ sauce
34. Building near a silo
35. Dr. of hip-hop
36. Eye the bull's-eye
37. Lose one's cool
38. Flavorful seed
40. Sought office
41. "Leaving ___ Vegas"
42. Passionate
46. Scruff of the neck
49. Roman wrap
51. Stadium cry
52. "Hold on ___!"
53. Scored perfectly on
54. Brownies' org.
55. That's partner
56. When doubled, a dangerous fly
57. Granola grain

DOWN

1. TV's Donahue
2. "___ Like It Hot"
3. Rip
4. Choirs may stand on them
5. Tennis champ Chris
6. Spelling contest
7. Rosetta ___
8. Attorney's profession
9. Dined
10. Faux ___ (blunder)
13. Rapid
19. Univ. sports org.
21. IHOP beverages
24. Family group
25. Pop singer Amos
26. In ___: harmonious
27. Counts up
28. Undercooked
29. The ___ of March
30. Letters after CD
33. Nap in Oaxaca
34. Rock group

36. Doctors' grp.

37. Event with floats

39. Baldwin and Guinness

40. Spreads unchecked

43. As a result

44. Cape Canaveral org.

45. "How about ___?!"

46. Cole who was "King"

47. Volcanic fallout

48. I. M. the architect

50. Halloween mo.

Solution on Page 311

ACROSS

1. ___ and turn
5. "Just a ___!" ("Hold on!")
8. Former mayor Giuliani
12. Not pro
13. In the ___ of luxury
14. Poet Pound
15. One and only
16. Timetable abbr.
17. Thailand's former name
18. Let us know, on an invitation
20. Goes on and on
21. Fashionably outdated
24. Holbrook of "Into the Wild"
25. Spanish houses
26. West Point students
29. Invite
30. Solar-system center
31. "I get it!"
33. Subject of a will
36. Challenged
38. Cowboy Rogers
39. Face-to-face exams
40. Bo of "10"
43. HS junior's test
45. Home furnishings chain
46. Shriver of tennis
47. 401(k) alternatives
51. Dryer outlet
52. "The Simpsons" shopkeeper
53. Chinese: prefix
54. Big fusses
55. Long. opposite
56. Frog's relative

DOWN

1. Prof.'s helpers
2. Yoko of "Double Fantasy"
3. City in Mo.
4. ___ Leone
5. Serb or Croat
6. Wyatt of the West
7. Life-saving skill, for short
8. Secondhand shop deal
9. Submachine guns
10. "Doggone it!"
11. Thanksgiving side dish
19. Morse Mayday
20. Young boy
21. Big TV maker
22. Lighten, as a burden
23. Sounds of disapproval
24. Liu Pang's dynasty
26. Stage signal
27. Scarlett's home
28. Writer-illustrator Silverstein
30. Pigpen
32. Product pitches
34. Alternatives to tricks
35. Fine

36. ___ good deed daily

37. Monet or Manet

40. Temperamental performer

41. ___ out (barely made)

42. Nevada city

43. Mama's partner

44. Pornography

46. Buddy

48. Brazilian port, for short

49. ___ for effort

50. Piece of turf

Solution on Page 311

ACROSS

1. Loch of lore
5. Sugar amt.
8. Drunk ___ skunk
11. Stew
12. Paper purchase
14. Boo-hoo
15. Country road
16. Boat paddles
17. NBC weekend comedy
18. Tom Sawyer author
20. Thick
22. Group of ships
24. ___ Angeles Dodgers
25. Tennis great Ivan
26. Scalawag
29. Like some stocks: abbr.
30. Dog days mo.
31. Sign of approval
33. Calm, cool, and collected
36. Craze
38. "48 Hours" network
39. Humor with a twist
40. Seaweed
43. Distribute, as shares
45. Rocker ___ Jovi
46. Breathing sound
48. Wal-___
51. "Green Acres" star Gabor
52. DVR pioneer
53. Lots and lots
54. "Game, ___, match!"
55. Did a marathon
56. ___ up (in the bag)

DOWN

1. Green Bay Packers' org.
2. End of an ___
3. Convicted criminal's punishment
4. Prepared, as tomatoes
5. "Star Trek": TNG counselor Deanna
6. Connery of 007 fame
7. Duffer's goal
8. Professional org.
9. Daughters' counterparts
10. "___ to leap tall buildings . . ."
13. Windows predecessor
19. Capital of GA
21. Emergency PC key
22. Showman Ziegfeld
23. Prince's "___ Go Crazy"
24. Fall behind
26. Be sorry
27. Comment on, as in a margin
28. Pork cut
30. Reply to a ques.
32. It breaks in the morning
34. "His Master's Voice" co.
35. Movie critic Roger

Puzzle 48

1
2
3
4
5
6
7
8
9
10
11
12
13
14
15
16
17
18
19
20
21
22
23
24
25
26
27
28
29
30
31
32
33
34
35
36
37
38
39
40
41
42
43
44
45
46
47
48
49
50
51
52
53
54
55
56

36. $1,000,000, for short
37. Inviting smells
40. Lincoln and Vigoda
41. Zero, on a court
42. Pesky flier
43. Thomas Edison's middle name
44. Trotsky or Uris
47. Tire fill
49. Use the oars
50. "Grand Ole Opry" network

Solution on Page 311

ACROSS

1. Straitlaced
5. "Bill & ___ Excellent Adventure"
9. Cup's edge
12. Currency on the Continent
13. Basic util.
14. Slippery, as a road
15. Calligraphers' supplies
16. From quite a distance
17. Actor Gibson
18. Stomach muscles
20. Tranquility
22. Clothing
25. Computer storage unit, informally
26. Winston Cup org.
27. Put into law
30. Transcript fig.
31. ___ flask (liquor container)
33. Flubbed
37. Pacific weather phenomenon
40. Losing tic-tac-toe line
41. Oklahoman
42. Upstream swimmer
45. Slice
46. Some IHOP drinks
47. Stuffed tortilla
49. Roadrunner's sound
53. Air safety grp.
54. "Like ___ not"
55. Lumberjacks' tools
56. "Wherefore ___ thou Romeo?"
57. Boston hoopster, for short
58. Sandwich seller

DOWN

1. Shar-___ (dog)
2. "Walk, don't ___!"
3. Annoy
4. Artwork made of tiles
5. Ad to lure you in
6. Worker in Santa's workshop
7. "Oh, what am I to do?"
8. Bug barrier
9. Prom night transportation
10. Frozen treats
11. Journalist Ernie
19. Push-up lingerie item
21. Links org.
22. Oscar-winning director Lee
23. 3M product
24. Ivan or Nicholas
28. Goatee's locale
29. Fork prong
32. ___ favor: please (Sp.)
34. CD-___
35. Like some dancers or pets
36. Present to Goodwill, e.g.
37. Accompany to a party
38. Baseball great Gehrig
39. Pretty good!

1	2	3	4		5	6	7	8		9	10	11
12					13					14		
15					16					17		
			18	19			20		21			
22	23	24				25						
26						27		28	29			
30								31			32	
	33		34	35	36	37	38	39				
			40			41						
42	43	44				45						
46				47	48			49	50	51	52	
53				54				55				
56				57				58				

42. Couch

43. Partially open

44. Future DA's exam

48. Maj.'s superior

50. Devon river

51. Sushi fish

52. Tire pressure meas.

Solution on Page 312

ACROSS

1. Reggae's Marley
4. "The Eagle ___ Landed"
7. Performed an aria
11. Farm output
13. Clairvoyant's claim
14. Blacken
15. Couturier Christian
16. "Do ___ say, . . ."
17. Marching ___ war
18. ". . . happily ever ___"
20. MGM mogul Marcus
21. TV studio light
24. Throaty utterance
26. Put out, as a fire
27. Motherly ministering, for short
28. "Raiders of the Lost ___"
31. Leers at
32. Vietnam's capital
34. Curtain holder
35. "30 Rock" network
38. Fund, as one's alma mater
39. Word-wise Webster
40. City known for its Heat
41. Art ___: geometric style
44. ___ pole
46. Jane who loved Mr. Rochester
47. ___ and aah
48. "Dear" advice columnist
52. Lunch or dinner
53. Intel org.
54. "___ of the Flies"
55. Spheres
56. Use a Singer
57. Exxon product

DOWN

1. "A–E" link
2. "It must be him, ___ shall die . . ."
   (Vikki Carr line)
3. Halloween greeting
4. Radiator emanation
5. State with confidence
6. Type of staircase
7. Where hair roots grow
8. "I get it," humorously
9. Thurmond of NBA fame
10. Expand
12. Heap kudos on
19. California raisin city
21. Ammonia has a strong one
22. Like a scrubbed space mission
23. "___ Lang Syne"
25. Plot
28. Forever ___ day
29. Kitchen or den
30. Fuzzy green fruit
33. Orwell's "___ Farm"

Solution on Page 312

36. Conductors' sticks
37. Opt for
39. Christmas carols
41. Test-driver's car
42. Watcher
43. Sea creature that moves sideways

45. Unfreeze
49. Where cranberries grow
50. Playtex product
51. Gridiron divs.

Solution on Page 312

ACROSS

1. Electrical resistance unit
4. Klutz's cry
8. ___ Club (discount chain)
12. Lawyer's payment
13. Take a chance with
14. Fast-food option
15. Enthusiast
16. "If all ___ fails . . ."
17. Gifts to the poor
18. Made a web
20. Bit of kindling
22. Catch red-handed
25. ___ firma
29. Like a court witness
34. Feel bad
35. ___ chi: martial art
36. Snake charmer's snake
37. Sick
38. Tarzan raiser
39. Some three-digit numbers
41. Despised
43. Shoulder enhancer
44. Plane assignment
47. Strikebreaker
51. Emily of etiquette
54. One drawn to a flame
57. Top poker card
58. Cheese with a moldy rind
59. Sky color, in Paris
60. Entertainer Zadora
61. HS seniors' exams
62. Eric of Monty Python
63. Not divisible by two

DOWN

1. Murders, mob-style
2. Messy pile
3. List from a waiter
4. Mine find
5. ___ and vinegar
6. Hissed "Hey!"
7. Depict unfairly
8. Thespian's platform
9. It merged with Time Warner
10. Famed movie studio
11. Shipwreck signal
19. Compass pt. opposite SSW
21. Cornell's home
23. Hangout for pinball wizards
24. Churlish chap
26. Police assault
27. Get one's dander up
28. "___ fair in love and war"
29. Mormon state
30. California wine valley
31. Cut calories
32. Honest ___ (presidential moniker)
33. Pitfall
40. Has too much

Puzzle 51

1
2
3
4
5
6
7
8
9
10
11
12
13
14
15
16
17
18
19
20
21
22
23
24
25
26
27
28
29
30
31
32
33
34
35
36
37
38
39
40
41
42
43
44
45
46
47
48
49
50
51
52
53
54
55
56
57
58
59
60
61
62
63

42. ___ Park, CO
45. Both: prefix
46. Spilled the beans
48. Crime chief
49. Citric ___
50. Drop of sweat
51. "FRONTLINE" airer
52. "Is it a boy ___ girl?"
53. Take a chair
55. ___ Aviv
56. Color

Solution on Page 312

ACROSS

1. Small pie
5. ___-of-the-moment
9. Part of CST
12. "That's clear"
13. Citrus fruit
14. Fallen space station
15. 1/500 of the Indianapolis 500
16. Part of RPI
17. Opposite WSW
18. Annual coll. basketball competition
20. 1950s candidate Stevenson
22. Accumulate
25. One with a halo
27. TV control abbr.
28. Maui dance
30. "Just the facts, ___"
33. "Got it, man"
35. Dashed
36. Willy of "Free Willy"
37. Mosquito repellent ingredient
38. Wildebeests
40. Friend in France
41. Sniffers
43. Lugged along
45. Involuntary twitch
47. Siesta
48. Boiling
49. Mock words of understanding
52. "Sesame Street" skills

56. Lode load
57. Diving bird
58. Jump
59. NBA tiebreakers
60. Funnyman Jay
61. Egotist's love

DOWN

1. Tiny Dickens boy
2. "___ was saying . . ."
3. Fam. member
4. Adolescents
5. Cut like a letter opener
6. Bowler's target
7. Vocal stumbles
8. Label anew
9. Suspect dishonesty
10. Fey of "30 Rock"
11. Eins + zwei
19. Sort of suffix
21. Wannabe recording star's tape
22. Enthusiastic
23. À la ___ (with ice cream)
24. Estranges
25. Arkin and Alda
26. Half of Mork's goodbye
29. Hankering
31. Very top
32. Old ___ (card game)
34. Classic Pontiacs

39. RR depot
42. Wee
44. Milky gems
45. "Scat!"
46. Dessert wine
47. "___, Nanette"
50. Weeding tool

51. Michael Douglas, to Kirk
53. Buzzer in a hive
54. Ore. neighbor
55. Beach lotion letters

Solution on Page 312

ACROSS

1. Hors d'oeuvre spread
5. PC alternative
8. Wastes, in mob slang
12. Was beholden to
13. Wed. follower
14. Rattling breath
15. Crooned
16. Big wine-holder
17. Chew, squirrel-style
18. Jekyll's bad side
19. Banjo virtuoso Fleck
21. Grassy clump
24. Foreword, for short
28. Spanish hero El ___
31. Yank out of bed
34. Kennel sound
35. Submachine gun
36. Gold bar
37. ___ in the sky
38. ___ appétit!
39. Gas additive
40. Aged
41. Decorate
43. Baltic or Bering
45. Write on metal
48. Feeling no pain
52. Sharp blow in karate
55. Ship's daily record
57. Deuce topper, in cards
58. "Mary ___ little lamb"
59. Resistance unit that sounds like a meditation word
60. Stevie Wonder's "___ She Lovely"
61. Nickname for Ford's Jones portrayal
62. Period
63. Job for Perry Mason

DOWN

1. One of the Spice Girls
2. On the road
3. Be inclined (to)
4. Borders
5. "The Real World" network
6. "Moby-Dick" captain
7. Adorable
8. Bach instrument
9. Air blower
10. State south of Ga.
11. Make a seam
20. Wee
22. "The ___ Express"
23. "___ Go Near the Water"
25. Misprint
26. Banister
27. ___ page (newspaper part)
28. Castro's country
29. Company with a crocodile logo
30. Pet on "The Flintstones"

Puzzle 53

1	2	3	4		5	6	7		8	9	10	11
12					13				14			
15					16				17			
18						19		20				
			21	22	23			24		25	26	27
28	29	30		31		32	33		34			
35				36					37			
38				39					40			
41			42				43		44			
			45		46	47			48	49	50	51
52	53	54			55		56		57			
58					59				60			
61					62				63			

32. "Yuck!"
33. Beans used for tofu
42. Settle, as a debt
44. Shenanigan
46. Blockhead
47. Sounds from Santa
49. Celestial bear
50. ___wear department
51. Data unit
52. "The Sweetheart of Sigma ___"
53. "Star Wars" pilot Solo
54. Not even
56. Prime meridian hrs.

Solution on Page 313

ACROSS

1. Attack with a knife
5. Certain boxing win, for short
8. Individually
12. Hydrant attachment
13. Male sheep
14. Yogi or Smokey
15. Despair's opposite
16. Weigh-___ (boxing rituals)
17. Opposite of out
18. Toothpaste holder
20. Sloppy
21. Biblical hymn
24. Snorkeling accessory
25. Makes yawn
26. Subdued color
29. Sutcliffe of the early Beatles
30. Makeshift shelter
31. Motor City gp.
33. "Cut that out!"
36. Michaels of "SNL"
38. Sales agent, briefly
39. Fire sign
40. TV show that had its Dey in court?
43. Gold deposit
45. Memorial news item
46. Bend over forward
47. Bart Simpson's brainy sister
51. Model Macpherson
52. Prohibit
53. "Holy moly!"
54. Gamblers place them
55. LP successors
56. Not for here

DOWN

1. Quiet!
2. This ___ shall pass
3. Nile biter
4. "___ Bailey"
5. Chicago paper, briefly
6. Welles role
7. Meditative sounds
8. Not present
9. Pod contents
10. Buffoons
11. The hunted
19. Hesitation sounds
20. Wrong: pref.
21. "Nova" network
22. Boozers
23. In ___ (going nowhere)
24. "___ chance!"
26. "___ Your Head On My Shoulder"
27. Continental money
28. Long and lean
30. Oft-swiveled joint
32. Pint-sized
34. Gives a speech
35. Bench for the faithful

36. '60s hallucinogen

37. Eggy dish

40. Leopold's codefendant

41. Having sufficient skill

42. Cheerful tune

43. Dumptruckful

44. Possesses

46. U.K. channel

48. "Can ___ now?"

49. Give in to gravity

50. Much about nothing

Solution on Page 313

ACROSS

1. Loony
5. Window frame
9. Tierra ___ Fuego
12. October's birthstone
13. ___ Pet
14. "___ Baba and the 40 Thieves"
15. TV's Nick at ___
16. Rock band boosters
17. Tombstone inscription
18. Compass part
20. Average marks
21. Opposite of post
22. "Lah-di-___!"
24. Nonpoetic writing
27. Biblical cry of praise
31. Aid for a stranded auto
32. Holey cheese
34. Nile snake
35. They'll show you the world
37. Face-valued, as stocks
39. "Science Guy" Bill
40. Fed. biomedical research agcy.
41. Does hip-hop
44. Beauty parlors
47. Birmingham's state: abbr.
48. Transport on rails
50. Breakfast, lunch, or dinner
52. ___ League
53. Wander about
54. Shells and bullets
55. "___ Boot" (1981 war film)
56. ___ of March
57. Nothing special

DOWN

1. The "N" in NCO
2. ___ arms (angry)
3. "Little Man ___" (Jodie Foster film)
4. Nods off
5. Weighing site
6. Alas!
7. Use a straw
8. Possesses
9. Challenge
10. Writer Wiesel
11. Loose ___ sink ships
19. Fancy, as clothes
20. Chinese tea
22. ___ and don'ts
23. Attack
24. School support org.
25. Decompose
26. "The ___ and the Pussycat"
27. "Killing Me Softly with ___ Song"
28. Catch forty winks
29. CIA relative
30. Mo. before May
33. Like early morning hours
36. Opposite of a ques.

38. Clarence of the Supreme Court

40. Tom, Dick, and Harry, e.g.

41. Surprise police tactic

42. Thomas ___ Edison

43. Picks up the tab

44. Put money in the bank

45. Nautilus captain

46. Snead and Spade

48. Prefix with cycle

49. Fishing stick

51. English lavatory

Solution on Page 313

ACROSS

1. Not near
4. Trio after "R"
7. Elitist
11. Three, on a sundial
12. Hatcher of "Desperate Housewives"
14. Whitish
15. They may administer IVs
16. Raggedy ___ (dolls)
17. Ready for business
18. Has the helm
20. Slap the cuffs on
22. Attorney F. ___ Bailey
23. 1950s prez
24. Sighing words
27. Great Leap Forward leader
28. Roast hosts, for short
31. Apple debut of 1998
32. "___! Humbug!"
33. Mary ___ little lamb
34. "The ___ Squad"
35. Old man
36. "___ Bitsy Spider"
37. Some boxing wins, for short
38. Vert. opposite
40. Viewpoints
43. Deficiency of red blood cells
47. World's longest river
48. Spruce up a manuscript
50. Lever on a casino "bandit"
51. "Must've been something ___"
52. ___ a good example
53. ___ v. Wade (landmark decision)
54. Major leaguers
55. Taste the soup
56. MSNBC rival

DOWN

1. Needle-bearing trees
2. "___ Too Proud to Beg" (1966 hit)
3. Get up
4. Gawk (at)
5. Uptight
6. Big coffee-holder
7. Mold's origin
8. Neck part
9. Bullfight cheers
10. Not straight
13. Old Testament prophet
19. Power co. product
21. "It's a Wonderful Life" studio
24. Intention
25. Med. group
26. Insane
27. Atlas feature
28. Place to wipe your shoes
29. PC inserts
30. Utter
32. Supervisors

122

Puzzle 56

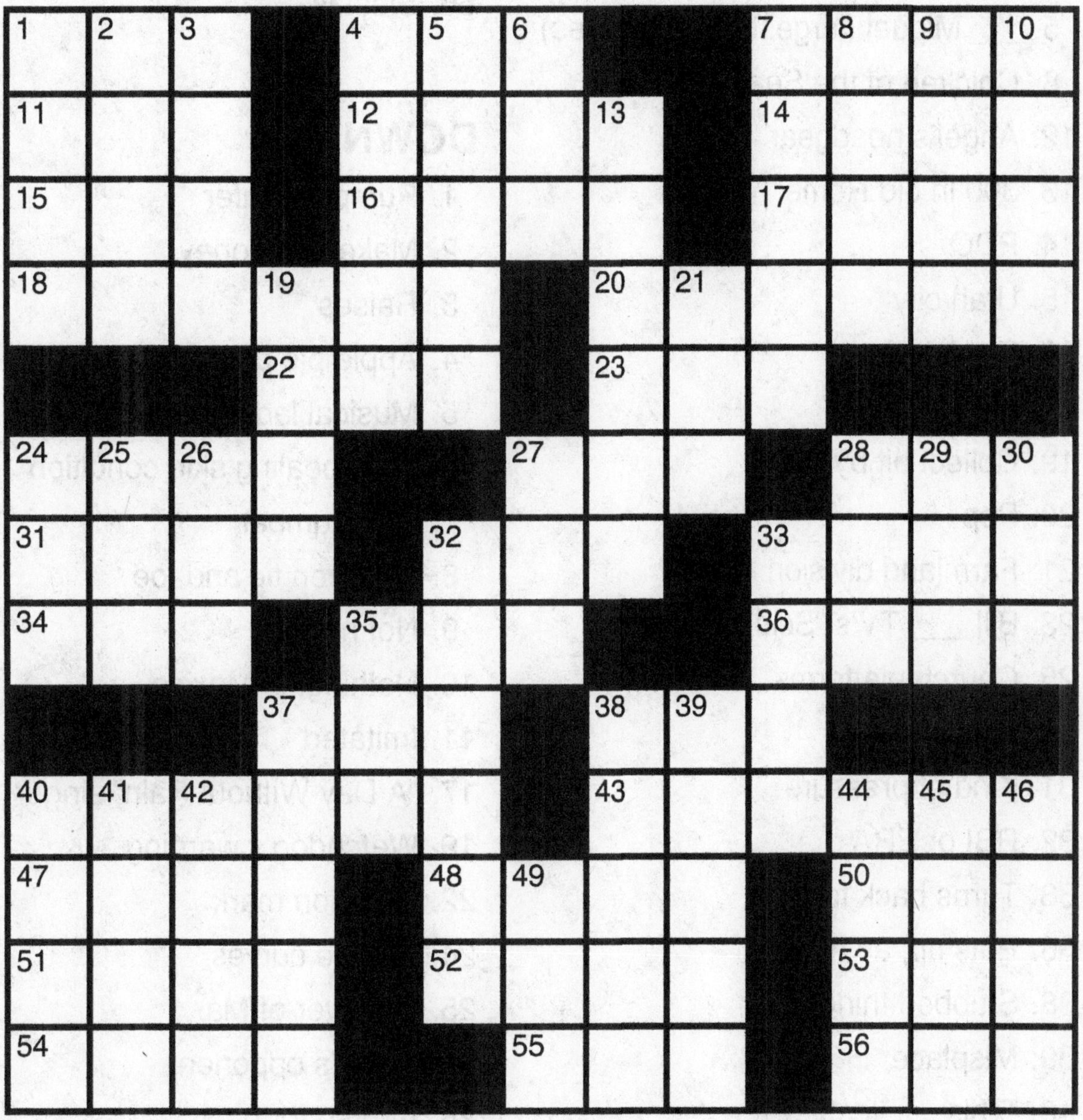

33. Put on the payroll
35. Money on a poker table
37. Prayers are often said on them
38. West Indies republic
39. Like draft beer
40. Barber's motion
41. Fibber
42. Voice above a tenor
44. Singer ___ Anthony
45. De-wrinkle
46. "You said it, brother!"
49. The ___ Moines Register

Solution on Page 313

ACROSS

1. Give the appearance of
5. ___ Miguel (largest of the Azores)
8. Chicken of the Sea product
12. Angel's headgear
13. 300 in old Rome
14. PDQ
15. Utah city
16. Predate
18. Ltr. holder
19. Collect bit by bit
20. Pop
21. Farmland division
23. Bill ___, TV's "Science Guy"
25. Church platforms
27. Studio stands
31. Kind of pressure
32. RBI or ERA
33. Turns back to zero
36. Puts up, as a tower
38. Stubbed thing
39. Misplace
40. "This ___ test . . ."
43. Give and take?
45. Recipe meas.
48. Hare racer
50. Lugosi of horror films
51. All alone
52. Cries at fireworks
53. "I smell ___!"
54. Ever and ___
55. "Who ___ the Dogs Out"
56. Siestas

DOWN

1. Pump or loafer
2. Make, as money
3. Raises
4. Apple pie partner?
5. Musical ladders
6. Unappealing skin condition
7. Gas number
8. Between tic and toe
9. Not new
10. Nothing, in Mexico
11. Imitated
17. "A Day Without Rain" singer
19. Watchdog's warning
22. Insertion mark
24. Double curves
25. Follower of Mar.
26. Grant's opponent
28. And so forth
29. Long.'s opposite
30. Ave. crossers
34. In ___ (completely)
35. Story that's "to be continued"
36. Most senior
37. ___ v. Wade
40. "___ small world!"

41. "Coming ___ to a theater near you"
42. Folkie Guthrie
44. Tennis great Arthur
46. Sharp blow
47. Butter servings

49. Coal delivery unit
50. Forbid

Solution on Page 314

ACROSS

1. Droops
5. Fall mo.
8. Calf's cry
11. The ___ thickens
12. Golf standard
13. "I'm too ___ for my shirt" (Right Said Fred lyric)
14. Jazz singer ___ James
15. DDT banner
16. Shade giver
17. Be kept waiting
20. ___ Vegas
21. "On ___ Majesty's Secret Service"
22. Dr. of gangsta rap
25. Actor Stephen
27. Traffic tie-up
31. Puts on
33. Ques. response
35. Venetian-blind part
36. Ripped off
38. Ruby, for one
40. Oohs and ___
41. Select, with "for"
43. Karl Marx's "___ Kapital"
45. Baseball's "Mr. October"
52. Gumbo vegetable
53. Singer ___ King Cole
54. Multinational currency
55. Lo ___ (noodle dish)
56. Adam's madam
57. Author Wiesel
58. "C'___ la vie!"
59. Profs.' helpers
60. Actions on heartstrings and pant legs

DOWN

1. Job detail, briefly
2. Kind of sax
3. Attend, as a party
4. Suddenly stop, as an engine
5. Middle of the ocean
6. Superhero's garment
7. Garbage
8. Simple
9. Skating jump
10. Nays' opposites
13. Backs of boats
18. Boater's blade
19. "For ___ a Jolly Good Fellow"
22. Shingle letters
23. Spoil
24. British musician Brian
26. Taiwanese-born director Lee
28. Cotton State: abbr.
29. Cheerleader's cheer
30. Capt.'s inferiors
32. Advertising catchphrase
34. Tranquilizes

Puzzle 58

37. Prefix with center or cycle

39. ___ and cheese

42. Basic belief

44. Trapshooting

45. ___ Beauty (apple variety)

46. Squeezes (out)

47. Sandpaper coating

48. Coffee, slangily

49. "Star Trek" navigator

50. Not a dup.

51. Negative votes

Solution on Page 314

ACROSS

1. U.S. soldiers
4. Chooses, with "for"
8. Fox or turkey follower
12. Fuse rating unit
13. Classic soft drink
14. Decorate anew
15. "The Raven" writer
16. Plant's beginning
17. Hawkeye player on "M*A*S*H"
18. Be pleasing (to)
20. ". . . fifteen miles on the ___ Canal"
22. Jolson and Jarreau
23. Maple leaf land
26. Blackboard material
29. "Dear old" guy
30. Lisa, to Bart Simpson
31. Rowing equipment
32. 90 degrees from vert.
33. Restroom door word
34. "For shame!"
35. Captain's record
36. West Pointer, e.g.
37. PLO leader
39. Computer screen, for short
40. Mechanical teeth
41. "___ Weapon" (Mel Gibson film)
45. They're sometimes inflated
47. Paid players
49. "Gimme ___!" (start of an Iowa State cheer)
50. Lassies' partners
51. Evict
52. Gibson or Blanc
53. Beat a hasty retreat
54. Golf ball props
55. Piggery

DOWN

1. Open the mouth wide
2. Springsteen's "___ Fire"
3. Raced
4. Bargain-hunter's favorite words
5. Equals
6. "For Whom ___ Bell Tolls"
7. Motorcycle attachment
8. Choo-choo
9. Set free
10. ___ man out
11. Generous ___ fault
19. Has dinner
21. "Far out!"
24. Wine and ___
25. Gofer: abbr.
26. Divan
27. Lion's home
28. Part of a telephone number
29. "Man's best friend"
32. Popular nightclub

33. Damon of "Good Will Hunting"
35. Hang back
36. Wave tops
38. "All That Jazz" director Bob
39. Neck and neck
42. Radio operators

43. Operating without ___ (taking risks)
44. Easter bloom
45. Santa's little helper
46. Guy's honey
48. Bemoan

Solution on Page 314

ACROSS

1. Sandy's barks
5. Partner of hem
8. Crib cry
11. Film spool
12. Move like molasses
13. Apple alternative
14. Winslet of "Titanic"
15. AARP part: abbr.
16. Classic auto
17. Went fast
18. Ike's initials
19. Salon applications
20. Poseidon's realm
22. Whisper sweet nothings
24. Speedometer letters
27. Go head to head
29. Up, on a map
33. Civil War soldier
34. Cove
36. Louvre Pyramid architect
37. Animal nose
39. To and ___
40. Cartographer's product
41. Rock's Fleetwood ___
43. Radio's PBS
45. Show appreciation at a
    performance
48. "___ Haw"
50. Big-ticket ___
54. "___ Master's Voice"

55. Uncontrollable movements
56. Father, to a baby
57. Birds ___ feather
58. Vegas machine
59. Divorcées
60. ___ pill (amphetamine)
61. Relatives
62. Go under

DOWN

1. Torah holders
2. Harvest
3. Celebration
4. Toboggans
5. Broke some ground
6. Ancient Mexican
7. Marry
8. Metal thread
9. One slain by Cain
10. Managed care grps.
12. Confer holy orders on
19. Guck or gunk
21. "Don't Cry for Me Argentina"
    musical
23. "___ of Old Smoky"
24. Bride's new title
25. Writing implement
26. "The Sopranos" network
28. North Pole toy-maker
30. LP speed
31. Lipton drink

130

32. Place to shoot from
35. Author Hemingway
38. Ballpark official
42. Hot dish with beans
44. Disney World attractions
45. Karate blow
46. Bygone picture weekly
47. Quickly, in memos

49. Supply-and-demand subj.
51. Cab
52. Garden of ___
53. Lone Ranger attire
55. Sound of disapproval

Solution on Page 314

ACROSS

1. Govt. property overseer
4. Uncertainties
7. Kitten call
10. City near Lake Tahoe
12. Dove's sound
13. Put away for a rainy day
14. Imminent danger warning
16. Docking spot
17. Vicious of the Sex Pistols
18. Shampoo step
19. Borden's cow
22. Excellent, in modern slang
24. Salespeople, briefly
25. "I've got it!"
28. Anatomical pouch
29. Machine shop tool
31. Approving head shake
33. End of two state names
35. Anderson of "WKRP in Cincinnati"
36. Christmas song
37. Apportions, with "out"
38. "The sky's the ___!"
41. Car-wash cloth
42. Mil. branch since 1947
43. Individually, on a menu
48. Michelin product
49. Break bread
50. Hawaiian neckwear
51. And so forth: abbr.
52. ___ Pepper
53. Animation frame

DOWN

1. Canine warning
2. Visualize
3. Common conjunction
4. Like summer tea
5. In favor of
6. Heavy drinker
7. Central street name
8. December 24 and 31
9. "___ #1!"
11. Desert spring
13. "Cut off your nose to ___ your face"
15. Tell whoppers
18. Scarce
19. Hosp. trauma centers
20. Metal that Superman can't see through
21. Pet advocacy org.
22. Flower feature
23. "Come again?"
26. Half hitch or bowline
27. Super-duper
29. Swag
30. Chowed down
32. Talk smack about
34. "Mack the ___"

35. Paper size

37. Singer Davis

38. Elizabethan instrument

39. "___ something I said?"

40. Cleopatra's love ___ Antony

41. Fully attentive

43. Donkey

44. Nut on a wheel

45. ___ center (community facility)

46. Cause for overtime

47. Class for U.S. immigrants

Solution on Page 315

ACROSS

1. Told a whopper
5. "Sesame Street" broadcaster
8. Porgy's love
12. Roof's edge
13. Singer Rawls
14. Words after shake or break
15. Ed of "Daniel Boone"
16. Egyptian reptile
17. Bed support
18. Chinese, e.g.
20. Old salts
21. Road no.
22. Last number in a countdown
24. Buying binge
27. Test for MA hopefuls
28. "Act your ___!"
31. Father's Day gift
32. Opening bets
34. Lemon meringue, for one
35. River blocker
36. "A Boy Named ___"
37. "One of ___ days . . ."
39. Sink, as the sun
40. Miss. neighbor
41. "Smooth Operator" singer
44. Regard with lust
47. Like the driven snow
48. Sup
49. Dry, as a desert
51. Slightly
52. "Ich ___ ein Berliner"
53. "___ in the Clowns"
54. Has the oars
55. Uplifting undergarment
56. Declares

DOWN

1. ___ & Perrins (sauce brand)
2. "___ Rock": Simon & Garfunkel hit
3. Nights before
4. Name of Tennessee's streetcar
5. 747, e.g.
6. Head honcho
7. Have an evening meal
8. Moisten the turkey
9. Fitzgerald of jazz
10. Scorch
11. Bilko et al.: abbr.
19. "Relax, soldier!"
22. Metallic rock
23. Hershey's competitor
24. Regular: abbr.
25. Zadora
26. Michael Stipe's band
27. Verizon forerunner
28. Companion of Tarzan
29. Enlisted soldiers, briefly
30. Extra-wide, at the shoe store
33. Cashew, for one

38. Give a hard time

39. Watermelon throwaways

40. MetLife competitor

41. Exchange jabs

42. Coupe or sedan

43. Quick ___ McGraw

44. Hibernation location

45. Carpeting calculation

46. Minuscule

48. Recede

50. Dentist's deg.

Solution on Page 315

ACROSS

1. Driver's lic. and such
4. It's hailed in cities
7. Former Iranian leader
11. VCR button
12. Wheels connection
14. Nightclub of song
15. Flightless bird
16. Quote authoritatively
17. Not at home
18. Boise's state
20. Sing in the Alps
22. Moon vehicle, for short
23. Roll-___ (some deodorants)
24. Hitting stats
27. Capote, for short
28. Pair
31. Cyclonic center
35. Berlin's land: abbr.
36. ___ Speedwagon
37. Egyptian goddess
38. Topeka is its cap.
39. It doesn't detonate
41. Lessen
43. Ryan of "Love Story"
46. Symbol on the Hollywood Walk of Fame
47. Turns bronze
49. Held first place
51. Film part
52. Nursery rhyme home of many children
53. Wide shoe designation
54. Twirl
55. Airport abbr.
56. Have a bawl

DOWN

1. Bitter feeling
2. Moore of "Disclosure"
3. Soviet ballistic missile
4. Secret stash
5. Self-evident truth
6. Sandwich initials
7. A whole slew
8. Inventor Elias
9. "Be ___ . . ." : "Help me"
10. Farm bale
13. Pooh's gloomy pal
19. "The Sun ___ Rises"
21. Burden of proof
24. Gas pump choice: abbr.
25. First-round pass
26. Comparative suffix
27. However, informally
28. Hair arrangements
29. Spoon-bender Geller
30. Mantra chants
32. Toga party site
33. Doctrines

34. Ocean motion
38. Singing Carpenter
39. Philanthropist
40. Al of Indy
41. Perched on
42. "___ Ha'i": "South Pacific" song
44. Sir ___ Guinness

45. Lecherous look
46. Upper class: abbr.
48. "I found it!"
50. Susan of "L.A. Law"

Solution on Page 315

ACROSS

1. "___ only as directed"
4. Bean curd
8. Impudent talk
12. Soccer Hall-of-Famer Hamm
13. Lay ___ the line
14. Pinhead
15. Interest amt.
16. Sushi bar soup
17. Start of a counting-out rhyme
18. Grand stories
20. Shelf
21. Bitterly pungent
23. "How much am ___?" (auction query)
25. "No ___, no gain"
26. Coagulate, as blood
27. Wilder's "___ Town"
30. Magician's cry
32. Crude shelter
34. QB's successes
35. "___! Who goes there?"
37. Lifeless
38. Chest rattle
39. Church donation
40. More rational
43. ___ Lodge (Motel 6 competitor)
45. Simba, for one
46. "Return of the Jedi" forest dweller
47. ___ out (withdraw)
50. "Garfield" dog
51. Marathon, e.g.
52. Slangy denial
53. Chicago star Richard
54. Pitcher Nolan
55. Flightless Aussie bird

DOWN

1. Baseball arbiter, for short
2. [Not my error]
3. Lunch joints
4. Fainthearted
5. Auricular
6. Paleontologist's find
7. One, to Juan
8. War horse
9. Wowed
10. Serenade
11. Eyelid woe
19. Bowling targets
20. Lo-fat
21. PDA entry
22. Check the age of
24. It goes with a nut
26. Anthracite, e.g.
27. Life-size replica's ratio
28. Salt Lake state
29. Went on horseback
31. "___ she blows!"
33. Tennis score

138

1	2	3		4	5	6	7		8	9	10	11
12				13					14			
15				16					17			
		18	19					20				
21	22					23	24					
25				26					27	28	29	
30			31			32		33				
34				35		36			37			
		38						39				
40	41	42				43	44					
45				46					47	48	49	
50				51					52			
53				54					55			

36. Wiggle room
38. Zellweger of "Bridget Jones's Diary"
39. Subway coin
40. Trudge through the mire
41. Capitol Hill helper
42. Dark film genre

44. ___-Cola
46. To ___ is human . . .
48. Cooking spray brand
49. Day of the wk.

Solution on Page 315

ACROSS

1. New Mexico town on the Santa Fe Trail
5. Prescription writers: abbr.
8. Some early PCs
12. ___ of measure
13. "___ la la!"
14. Christmas carol
15. It may be spun around a campfire
16. JFK's predecessor
17. Move to and fro
18. Lenin's land, for short
19. "___ can you see . . ."
21. "Wayne's World" negative
24. Big mess
28. Waldorf-___ Hotel
32. Discarded metal
33. Cousin of calypso
34. Make fun of
36. Set afire
37. Mischievous sprite
39. Harrison Ford's "Star Wars" role
41. Bee injury
42. '60s muscle car
43. Puts down
46. There's ___ day dawning
50. Pleasant
53. Near the center of
55. Capital of Italy
56. Frost or Burns
57. Computer's core, briefly
58. Satan's work
59. Laments
60. Fire residue
61. Pub missile

DOWN

1. "Swan Lake" skirt
2. Santa ___ (hot California winds)
3. Fixes a squeak
4. Canned heat
5. Hip, in the '60s
6. Extinct bird
7. "___ a Lady" (Tom Jones hit)
8. On the same wavelength
9. Violist's need
10. "Cry ___ River"
11. Family Stone frontman
20. Concurrence
22. Sandinista leader Daniel
23. Common Father's Day gift
25. Singer Guthrie
26. Pass alternative
27. ___ no good
28. Venomous snakes
29. Playlet
30. Curbside call
31. "That feels so-o-o good!"
35. ___ Harbor, Long Island
38. Small bays

140

40. Flew high

44. Family rec. facility

45. Drinks slowly

47. Exploding star

48. Dubai dignitary

49. Whip mark

50. "Fresh Air" airer

51. Debtor's note

52. So-so grade

54. Obviously!

Solution on Page 316

ACROSS

1. ___ and feathers
5. King beaters
9. Sunday seat
12. Tropical fever
13. Letterman, to friends
14. Luau instrument, informally
15. . . . ___ and not heard
16. Repeated
18. "___ we now our gay apparel"
20. Lucy of "Kill Bill"
21. Cut, as prices
24. Antiquated exclamation
28. Itsy bit
29. Golden touch king
33. Topper of "j"
34. I'd like to buy ___, Pat
35. Chest bone
36. "The Simpsons" bartender
37. Leo's studio
38. Colorado ski town
40. One ___ million
41. Mexican moolah
43. Computer-chip maker
45. It's between Can. and Mex.
47. Fighter with Fidel
48. Strong steam-brewed coffee
52. Not hard
56. Eisenhower nickname
57. Small-size bed
58. Heading on a list of errands
59. Racehorse, slangily
60. Parts of a min.
61. Junk e-mail

DOWN

1. Coll. helpers
2. A dog's ___ (long spell)
3. Wish it weren't so
4. Dispatches
5. Tennis score after deuce
6. Meower
7. Stuntman Knievel
8. Ongoing TV show
9. "To ___ it mildly . . ."
10. Squeeze (out)
11. Say, "I do"
17. Mo. before Labor Day
19. Electrical unit
21. Post office purchase
22. Actress Jessica
23. John or John Quincy
25. Allow in
26. Blackmore's "Lorna ___"
27. Pilfer
30. Tax agency: abbr.
31. Potato chip accompaniment
32. Penny prez
38. Desirable qualities
39. Medical research agcy.

Puzzle 66

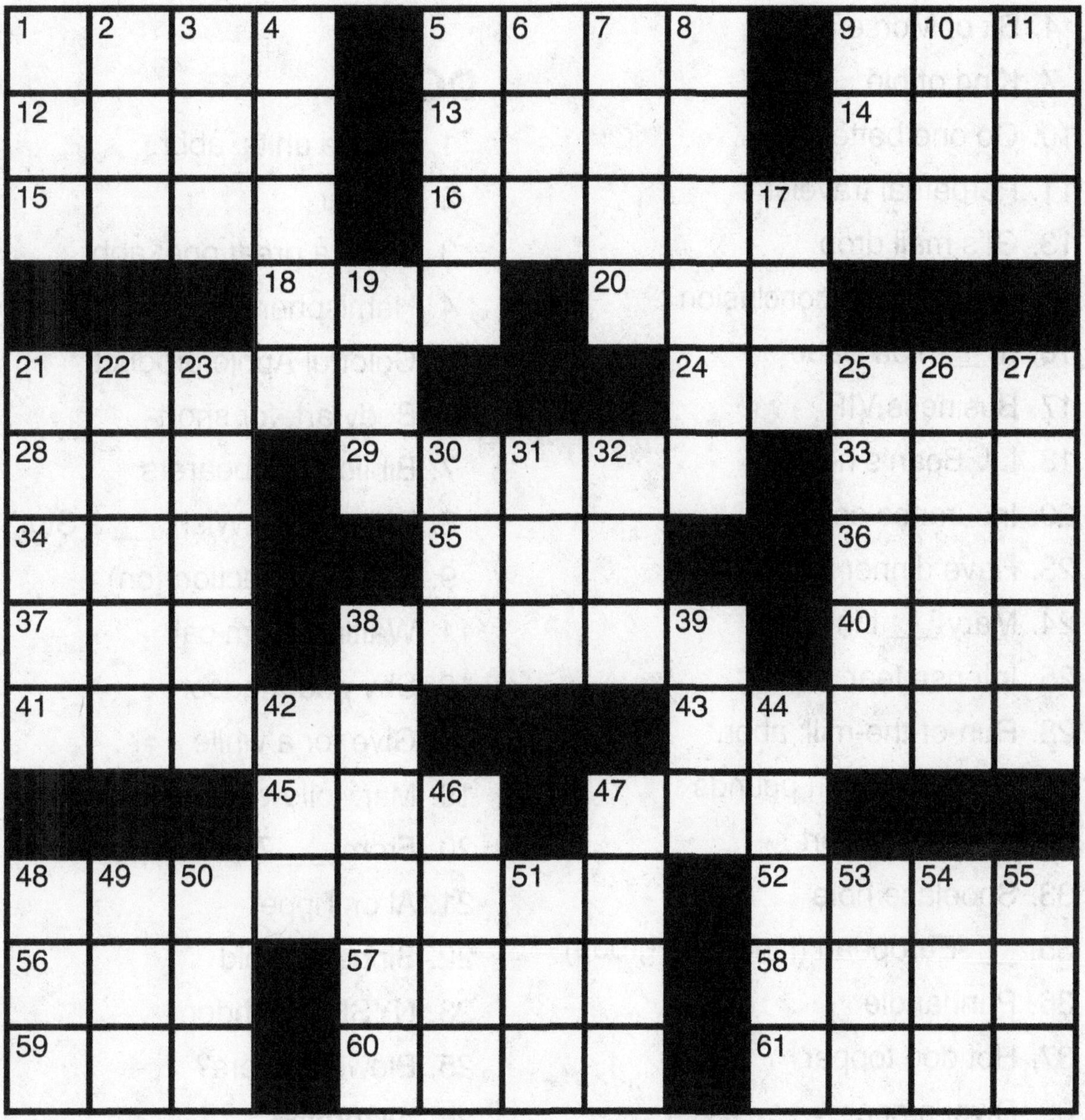

1
2
3
4
5
6
7
8
9
10
11
12
13
14
15
16
17
18
19
20
21
22
23
24
25
26
27
28
29
30
31
32
33
34
35
36
37
38
39
40
41
42
43
44
45
46
47
48
49
50
51
52
53
54
55
56
57
58
59
60
61

42. "And now a word from ___ sponsor"
44. Hatchlings' homes
46. ". . . ___ forgive those who trespass . . ."
47. Swindles
48. Ich bin ___ Berliner
49. Calypso cousin
50. Pin for hanging
51. [Intentionally so written]
53. Alley in the comics
54. Govt. Rx watchdog
55. Adventure hero Swift

Solution on Page 316

ACROSS

1. Chinese food additive
4. Bit of Morse code
7. Kind of pie
10. Go one better
11. Perpetual traveler
13. GI's mail drop
14. Inconclusive conclusion
16. "I ___ You Babe"
17. Business VIP
18. L.L.Bean's home
20. Insurance sellers
23. Have dinner
24. Mary ___ Lincoln
25. Intense fear
28. Run-of-the-mill: abbr.
29. Parts of British pounds
31. Club ___ resort
33. Shoelace hole
35. ___-European (language group)
36. Panhandle
37. Hot dog topper
39. Diver's gear
42. Cry like a baby
43. ___ favor (please, in Spanish)
44. Get out of the way
49. Stimpy's cartoon pal
50. Dine at home
51. Woman of habit?
52. Gridiron gains: abbr.
53. Not behaving well
54. Oct. follower

DOWN

1. Range units: abbr.
2. Tippler
3. 4.0 is a great one: abbr.
4. Hemispherical roofs
5. Colorful Apple product
6. Body art, for short
7. Biblical gift bearers
8. "When You Wish ___ a Star"
9. Shower affection (on)
11. Waiting room call
12. Shy and modest
15. Give for a while
19. Mar. follower
20. From ___ Z (totally)
21. Al or Tipper
22. Singer Arnold
23. NYSE watchdog
25. Blowup letters?
26. All: prefix
27. Johnny Bench's team
29. "I beg of you"
30. Brain scan, briefly
32. Play-___ (kiddie clay)
34. Flow back
35. Misfortunes
37. Swift

38. McGregor of "Star Wars" films
39. Nimble
40. Like some dorms
41. Vases
42. Alpha, ___, gamma
45. File folder feature
46. Roadside rest

47. Twosome
48. Ltr. container

Solution on Page 316

ACROSS

1. Fixes, as a fight
5. Annoys
9. Nev. clock setting
12. Parcel of land
13. ". . . so shall ye ___"
14. "Strange Magic" grp.
15. Sea swallow
16. Eight: Comb. form
17. On the ___ (at large)
18. Its symbol is Sn
20. Superman portrayer Christopher
22. Short cheer
25. Alpine dwelling
28. "Four score and seven years ___
     . . ."
29. One of 18 on a golf course
30. Greenish-blue
34. Three-piece suit piece
36. Tach reading
37. Medal recipient
38. Colon's meaning, in analogies
39. Pulled the trigger
41. Youthful fellow
42. Seas
44. Scale amts.
45. Macintosh maker
48. Turntable turners, briefly
50. Coffee, in slang
51. Ten: pref.

54. Part of IBM
58. "The Ice Storm" director ___ Lee
59. Openly declare
60. Stratagem
61. Illiterates' marks
62. ___ to riches
63. British submachine gun

DOWN

1. Lab-maze runner
2. ___ cream
3. Dog's warning
4. Shipped
5. Old name for a locomotive
6. Amusement, for short
7. Kit ___ bar
8. Tire in the trunk
9. Brazilian soccer star
10. Many a Balkan
11. Large volume
19. "I," as in Innsbruck
21. ___ A Sketch: drawing toy
22. Sitarist Shankar
23. Matures
24. Party giver
26. Beta preceder
27. They protect car buyers
31. Rebel ___ (Confederate battle cry)
32. United ___ Emirates
33. Nonverbal OKs

146

35. Screwdriver, for one
40. Recipe abbreviation
43. Closet wood
45. Stronger than dirt sloganeer
46. Johnnycake
47. Cribbage markers
49. Knights' titles

52. Zsa Zsa's sister
53. Machine tooth
55. Cashew or filbert
56. China's Mao ___-tung
57. NFL Hall-of-Famer Dawson

Solution on Page 316

ACROSS

1. Mohawk-sporting actor
4. Org. for Tiger Woods
7. Pork serving
11. Sic a lawyer on
12. On a pension: abbr.
14. Ear part
15. Old telecom giant
16. "This one's ___"
17. Clapton who sang "Layla"
18. Ditty
20. Whooping birds
22. Parisian pancake
24. Skirt opening
25. Yours and mine
26. Passes, as time
29. '50s pres.
30. Snoozer's sound
31. "Charlie's Angels" costar Lucy
33. Teach
35. Lairs
36. Indicator of rpm
37. Knights' wives
38. Classify
41. ___ Ruth
42. Airshow stunt
43. Subj. for Keynes
45. "Car Talk" network
48. Short skirt
49. "Stop it!"
50. Beachgoer's shade
51. Pond scum component
52. Deep distress
53. Al Green's "___-La-La"

DOWN

1. No ___ (Chinese menu notation)
2. Groove
3. Balanced on the brink
4. Inclined
5. Trait carrier
6. Green machine?
7. Golf shoe features
8. ___ of plenty
9. New York theater award
10. Chest muscles, briefly
13. Announce
19. Downs' opposite
21. Ready to pick
22. $-due mail
23. Ill-mannered
24. Laziness
26. Made into law
27. Strunk and White's "The ___ of Style"
28. Trig. term
30. Sign of injury
32. ___ Enterprise
34. Perfect world
35. Perfume amount

37. Author of "The Divine Comedy"
38. ___ mater
39. Flowerpot filler
40. Ballad, for example
41. Pro ___ (like some legal work)
44. Moo maker

46. Oom-___
47. Genetic material, for short

Solution on Page 317

ACROSS

1. Carter and Grant
5. Nile viper
8. Self-satisfied
12. Song for two
13. Arrived lifeless, briefly
14. Actress Spelling
15. It's ___ big mistake!
16. First mo.
17. ___-to-riches
18. Peach ___ (dessert)
20. Small size
22. Carry with effort
24. Ullmann or Tyler
25. Prohibited
29. Oyster's prize
33. Hive dweller
34. Telly network
36. Loving murmur
37. Roadside stopover
40. Prominent, as a feature
43. "Chocolate" dog
45. "What's up, ___?"
46. Pictures on a screen
49. More friendly
53. "___ just me, or . . .?"
54. Stimpy's canine pal
56. Googly-eyed Muppet
57. Zero
58. Squeal (on)
59. Japanese wrestling
60. & & &
61. Fireplace residue
62. Furniture wood

DOWN

1. Economist Smith
2. Stubborn beast
3. Holler
4. Horse house
5. Word that modifies a noun: abbr.
6. Suds maker
7. Group of experts
8. Try hard
9. Castle encircler
10. Feel the ___
11. Enlistees
19. Eighth mo.
21. Waiter's reward
23. Talk and talk and talk
25. "Big Blue"
26. Zodiac lion
27. Allow
28. Many oz.
30. King topper
31. Nancy Reagan's son
32. Auction unit
35. Contemptible fellow
38. Makes very happy
39. Time delay

41. Creepy Chaney
42. Most chilling
44. Quotable Yogi
46. "The heat ___!"
47. Matter topper?
48. Salty seven
50. Hint

51. Poet Lazarus
52. Piece next to a knight
53. Put ___ good word for
55. The highest degree

Solution on Page 317

ACROSS

1. eBay action
4. Transfixed
8. Snaky swimmers
12. Reverent respect
13. Do as directed
14. Lewd material
15. Research room
16. "I've ___ had!"
17. Harbor vessels
18. Words in an analogy
20. Sampras of tennis
22. 76ers' org.
25. Man with morals
29. "A ___ Named Desire"
34. West Bank grp.
35. "Annabel Lee" poet
36. You're ___ friends
37. Internet pop-ups, e.g.
38. Former California fort
39. Volunteer State
41. Kind of pool or wave
43. See ___ glance
44. ___ carotene
47. "But ___, there's more!"
51. Order to Fido
54. Gung-ho
57. . . . see hide ___ hair of
58. Minimum points
59. Morse ___
60. Prefix for light
61. Wise birds
62. Deuces
63. "Play It Again, ___"

DOWN

1. Indonesian island
2. "___ a Teenage Werewolf"
3. Money you owe
4. Hold up, as a bank
5. Pres. Lincoln
6. Chick's sound
7. Newcastle-upon-___, England
8. Cosmetician Lauder
9. Big bird
10. Big galoot
11. Kin of aves.
19. Lonely number
21. Dartboard, for one
23. John, Paul, George, or Ringo
24. "Look ___ I'm Sandra Dee"
26. Resorts with springs
27. Merrie ___ England
28. Sit for a portrait
29. "You missed a ___!"
30. Spelling of "Beverly Hills, 90210"
31. Actor Foxx
32. Not pro
33. Tolstoy's "___ Karenina"
40. Logger's tool

42. Bottomless pit

45. Discretion

46. Confess

48. Aardvarks' fare

49. Davenport's state

50. Quick haircut

51. Word with pitch or mo

52. AAA offering

53. Leatherworker's puncher

55. Solemn wedding words

56. ___ Moines

Solution on Page 317

ACROSS

1. Faucet sound
5. "Ay, there's the ___"
8. Tell all
12. Judge's attire
13. . . . for what ___ man . . .
14. Suffix with million
15. Not an abstainer
16. Rock's ___ Lobos
17. Trillion: pref.
18. Courage and fortitude
20. "Pipe down!"
22. Venomous snake
24. Common URL ender
27. Honeydew, e.g.
31. On the line
33. Victor's cry
34. Where surgeons work: abbr.
35. Level
36. Soup cracker
38. Ownership papers
39. Explosive letters
40. Mean-spirited
42. Winter mo.
43. Have a connection
48. Like a carbon copy
51. Dehydrated
53. Sailor's greeting
54. Elem. school groups
55. Delivery docs, for short
56. ___ of Man
57. Fly like a butterfly
58. Tiny criticism
59. Rocker Rundgren

DOWN

1. Percussion instrument
2. Thorny flower
3. Skeptic's comment
4. Sassy
5. Irritated
6. Mil. entertainment group
7. Droopy-eared hounds
8. Soaking site
9. Untruth
10. Train schedule abbr.
11. Arthur of "The Golden Girls"
19. PC linking acronym
21. Mins. and mins.
23. Tempts fate
24. Stalagmite site
25. Approved
26. The "M" in YMCA
27. "Gorillas in the ___"
28. McGregor of "Trainspotting"
29. Light, happy tune
30. Toronto's loc.
32. Titleist supporter
34. Endlessly
37. Pig ___ poke

Puzzle 72

38. Redhead maker
41. Lovers' rendezvous
42. "Surely you ___!"
44. Café au ___
45. "I get it," humorously
46. Informed
47. Got a good look at
48. Tanning-lotion letters
49. U.S./U.K. divider
50. ___ tai (rum drink)
52. Hitter's stat

Solution on Page 317

ACROSS

1. Vintners' vessels
5. Recedes, as the tide
9. "This means ___!"
12. Jim Croce's "___ a Name"
13. Stuck in ___
14. "___ Yankee Doodle Dandy"
15. Sierra Club co-founder
16. Lee of cakes
17. Family room
18. Runs off to marry
20. Student's book
21. Nothing
22. Disco ___ of "The Simpsons"
24. Maxim
27. Cowboy hat
31. Gift decoration
32. German wine valley
34. "___ were you . . ."
35. Goes ballistic
37. Tithe amount
39. Baseball's Griffey
40. Film critic Reed
41. Fix, at the vet's
44. Least cooked
47. "___ Abner"
48. Fashionable
50. Kitchen or bath
52. School of thought
53. Fool
54. Oom-pah instrument
55. Some univ. instructors
56. The Beatles' "___ a Woman"
57. Hightailed it

DOWN

1. ___ and vigor
2. Chills and fever
3. Slave away
4. Brawny
5. Artist's prop
6. Bosom companions
7. Prickly seedcase
8. Depot: abbr.
9. Not narrow
10. Visa alternative, briefly
11. Angry outburst
19. South Dakota's capital
20. Egyptian boy king
22. Train stop: abbr.
23. Ride a seesaw
24. Tummy muscles
25. Buck's mate
26. Great respect
27. Vicious or Caesar
28. Break a commandment
29. Frequently
30. Disease research org.
33. Rooster's mate
36. Cloud backdrop

Puzzle 73

1 2 3 4 5 6 7 8 9 10 11
12 13 14
15 16 17
18 19 20
21 22 23
24 25 26 27 28 29 30
31 32 33 34
35 36 37 38
39 40
41 42 43 44 45 46
47 48 49 50 51
52 53 54
55 56 57

38. Puts forth, as effort
40. Indy 500 and others
41. Thin cut
42. Leaning Tower home
43. Charity
44. Ready to harvest
45. Progresso product
46. Fit ___ tied
48. S&L offerings
49. "Come again?"
51. Irate

Solution on Page 318

ACROSS

1. Slow, musically
6. Soak (up)
9. "Evil Woman" rock group
12. Mr. T series, with "The"
13. Arrow's path
14. "Put a ___ on it!"
15. Syrup flavor
16. "___ Pepper's Lonely Hearts Club Band"
17. Acted as a guide
18. They give people big heads
20. Construction ___
21. ___-Atlantic
24. Lincoln or Vigoda
25. Eyeshade
26. Dr. who discovered Eminem
27. 1950s Ford flop
29. Perceives
32. Declare to be true
36. Something to lend or bend
38. Pontiac in a '60s hit song
39. Battleship blast
42. Vehicle
44. Day___: pigment brand
45. Family-history diagram
46. Converse
48. Stephen of "Michael Collins"
49. Drink cooler
51. Wood finish
55. Young' ___ (kids)
56. Hosp. workers
57. Grace under pressure
58. Rat-a-___ (drum sound)
59. ___ in the bag!
60. Water-balloon impact sound

DOWN

1. On the ___ (escaping)
2. One ___ time
3. Exerciser's unit
4. Battering wind
5. End of the Greek alphabet
6. Spoke impudently to
7. Not edu or com
8. Meas. of interest
9. New York Harbor's ___ Island
10. "Would I ___ you?"
11. More eccentric
19. More than fat
20. River deposit
21. Hosp. workers
22. Feeling of rage
23. Lair
25. Dog doc
28. Jazz singer Vaughan
30. File menu option
31. British rocker Brian
33. ___ foo yung
34. Gateway Arch city: abbr.

158

35. "The Man Who Knew ___ Much"
37. Passwords provide it
39. Walk proudly
40. Boxing venue
41. Fewest
43. Talks hoarsely
47. Semi-convertible auto roof

49. Uganda's Amin
50. Computer monitor: abbr.
52. Feel under the weather
53. It ___ far far better thing . . .
54. What's left after deductions

Solution on Page 318

ACROSS

1. Bangkok citizen
5. Back talk
8. Air passage
12. Hardwood trees
13. USAF part
14. Arthur of tennis
15. Exodus author Leon
16. Garbage bag securer
17. Astronaut Armstrong
18. Professor's security blanket
20. "Stars and Stripes Forever" composer
22. Listening organ
23. Weep loudly
24. Poor movie rating
28. Reddish hair dye
32. 24 hours
33. Meadow
35. Look through the crosshairs
36. Like Georgia Brown
39. Home of the Braves
42. Retrieve
44. Stranded motorist's need
45. Scarecrow stuffing
47. Passes, as a law
51. ___ or less (approximately)
52. PC maker
54. Stir up
55. Dirty reading
56. Easy mark
57. Birdbrain
58. Bee ___ ("Stayin' Alive" singers)
59. Big bang initials
60. Mulligan, for one

DOWN

1. Speak highly of
2. Loser to the tortoise
3. Having the same properties
4. Debate topics
5. Side-to-side
6. The Third
7. Reporters
8. River in a Strauss waltz
9. Depletes, with "up"
10. Pet that's a plant
11. ___ Aviv
19. Lab animal
21. Amazed audience utterance
24. Has too much of a bad thing
25. Backwoods refusal
26. Needle part
27. New Deal agcy.
29. One of the Bobbsey twins
30. Word with pick or wit
31. "I ___ Rock" (Simon & Garfunkel hit)
34. Take a shot at
37. Marsh birds

160

38. Alternative to coffee

40. "Man of a Thousand Faces" Chaney

41. Grammys, e.g.

43. Chubby Checker's dance

45. "___ Like It Hot"

46. Not made up

48. Crotchety oldster

49. Alabama's Crimson ___

50. Like molasses

51. No ___ (Chinese menu phrase)

53. Prohibition

Solution on Page 318

ACROSS

1. Lingerie item
4. Copied
8. Lose, as skin
12. Co. in a 2001 merger with Time Warner
13. Halliwell of the Spice Girls
14. Put blacktop on
15. Elm and Main: abbr.
16. Old horses
17. Gershwin and others
18. Agree
21. Cannery ___
22. ___ Z
23. "Now ___ this!"
25. Explosive initials
26. Gun lobby, briefly
29. Jackie Gleason role in "The Hustler"
33. Come-___ (inducements)
34. Star pitcher
35. ___ out a living (barely scrapes by)
36. Kind of: suff.
37. ___-K (toddlers' school)
38. Carnival confection
43. Shrill barks
44. Mary's pet
45. Holiday preceder
47. Creme-filled cookie
48. Old radio's "___ 'n' Andy"
49. Desire
50. Part of a bottle
51. Apartment payment
52. Reverse of WNW

DOWN

1. Some coll. degrees
2. Campus military org.
3. Distant finishers
4. A Nixon veep, last name
5. Bog material
6. Therefore
7. Aloof
8. A Nixon veep, first name
9. Cause injury to
10. Perón and Gabor
11. ___ Plaines, Ill.
19. "September ___" (Neil Diamond hit)
20. Blues singer James
23. Patient care gp.
24. One, in Bonn
25. Pedal digit
26. Unaided sight
27. Hwy.
28. Sure-footed work animal
30. "___ of Eden"
31. Learned one
32. Plant with fronds
36. Consoling phrase
37. Blue Ribbon brewer

38. Give a darn
39. Oil grp.
40. Moniker
41. "Get the lead out!"
42. Designer ___ Saint Laurent
43. Hither and ___
46. WSW's reverse

Solution on Page 318

ACROSS

1. Two-___ paper towels
4. Ft. above sea level, to a pilot
7. Former Iranian ruler
11. Old Olds car
12. Bull's-eye hitter
14. It's a race to break it
15. Acorn producer
16. Andy Taylor's TV son
17. Molecule component
18. Nasty looks
20. Pecan or cashew
22. Flying geese formation
23. Daubs
27. Assistants
30. Get-up-and-go
31. Soak up gravy
32. Scheme
33. Billy the ___
34. Regarding
35. Cherry seed
36. Word with gender or generation
37. Stanford-___ test
38. Spring or summer
40. Skedaddled
41. May and June: abbr.
42. Lure into crime
46. Big cat
49. "___ boy!"
51. "Cat ___ Hot Tin Roof"
52. Downhill aids
53. ___ splints (jogger's woe)
54. "Hulk" director Lee
55. Former "Entertainment Tonight" cohost John
56. Pro's vote
57. Daisy or Fannie

DOWN

1. ___ and cons
2. Low in fat
3. Oxen's harness
4. Loves to pieces
5. Expire, as a subscription
6. One less than quadri-
7. Michigan or Minnesota
8. Stetson or sombrero
9. Mil. address
10. Anti-fray border
13. ___ up (got nervous)
19. Tied
21. Ref.'s relative
24. Organization: abbr.
25. Mechanical routine
26. Dick and Jane's dog
27. iPhone downloads
28. Tennis great Nastase
29. Spreadsheet contents
30. Dot on a die
33. Auntie Em's home

164

34. "___ it the truth!"

36. Gunk

37. ___ split

39. Huge hit

40. Knot again

43. Wander

44. The "I" of "The King and I"

45. Beep with a beeper

46. Winter hrs. in L.A.

47. Don Ho's plunker

48. Prefix with place or print

50. "Honor ___ father and . . ."

Solution on Page 319

ACROSS

1. "___ my way"
5. "This weighs a ___!"
8. Tater
12. Walking stick
13. Gardner of "The Night of the Iguana"
14. ___ of the party
15. Letter accompanier: abbr.
16. Five-sided figure
18. Deli loaves
19. Train track
20. Saudi export
23. Hue
27. Knife or fork
31. Beauty mark
32. Scott Joplin tune
33. Assumed name
36. Neighbor of Wyo.
37. Olympic sled
39. Made happy
41. Lightning and thunder event
43. CD predecessors
44. Frees (of)
47. Fly into the wild blue yonder
51. Words with a handshake
55. "What's gotten ___ you?"
56. Straight ___ arrow
57. Printer's measures
58. Tipplers
59. Former Speaker Gingrich
60. Club ___ (resort)
61. Some nest eggs

DOWN

1. Cake finisher
2. Quite a few
3. Fairy tale starter
4. South Africa's Mandela
5. Beer keg insert
6. "Roger, ___ and out!"
7. Grandmother, affectionately
8. Zigzag skiing event
9. ___ out (overeat)
10. Mysterious saucer
11. Room with an easy chair
17. ___ Tac (breath freshener)
21. This ___ test
22. Capp's "___ Abner"
24. Lane of The Daily Planet
25. Ye ___ Shoppe
26. "___ my lips!"
27. Internet addresses
28. Drawn tight
29. Breakfast brand
30. Place to apply gloss
34. The whole shebang
35. Autumn mo.
38. Straying
40. St. Francis of ___

42. Central
45. Judge to be
46. "___ Time, Next Year"
48. ___ about (circa)
49. "___ girl!"
50. Flagmaker Betsy
51. James Bond creator Fleming
52. When doubled, a nasty fly
53. Toothed tool
54. It was dropped in the '60s

Solution on Page 319

ACROSS

1. Set fire to
5. Satisfied sigh
8. Manx or Siamese
11. Pester
13. It's south of Ga.
14. Drop of golden sun
15. Sawyer of TV
16. Sam ___ (Dr. Seuss character)
17. Suffix with west
18. Puts on TV
20. Brother of Curly and Shemp
21. Just a ___ (slightly)
24. Mouse sighter's cry
25. Barbie's beau
26. Pencil end
29. Amazement
31. Fender flaws
32. "Laughing" animal
36. Brown truck co.
38. Neighbor of Croatia
39. Prince, to a king
41. Suit ___ T
43. Crime lab evidence, briefly
44. Attack command to Fido
45. Start for Rooter or tiller
47. Picnic intruder
48. I'd rather not
49. Noodles
54. High card
55. Gobbled down
56. Dirty campaign tactic
57. Wager
58. Money roll
59. Mix (up)

DOWN

1. Not good
2. Prefix with cycle or sex
3. Genetic carrier
4. Smoking or ___? (waiter's query)
5. Blazing
6. Juneau's state
7. Sandwich meat
8. ___ de menthe
9. Home run king Hank
10. Newcastle's river
12. Vote of support
19. Suffix with bombard
21. Hall-of-Famer Williams
22. "You ___ So Beautiful"
23. Quarterback Marino
25. Florida isles
27. Stupefy
28. Sixth-sense letters
30. "___ goes there?"
33. Finish
34. Writer Anaïs
35. Motorists' org.
37. Rock layers

38. Mammal that sleeps upside-down
39. "___ you asked . . ."
40. Eight-member ensemble
42. Expressed wonder
44. Swedish car
46. Photo ___ (picture-taking times)
48. No, slangily

50. Early hrs.
51. Filming site
52. ___ chi
53. Part of ETA

Solution on Page 319

ACROSS

1. Place to exchange rings
6. Snakelike fish
9. Doctrine: suff.
12. Point-and-click gadget
13. CAT scan alternative
14. Na Na lead-in
15. Long, drawn-out stories
16. Lens protector
17. We ___ to please
18. What the "ten" of "hang ten" refers to
20. Santa ___ (city in California)
21. Wide of the mark
24. Membership charge
25. Top fighter pilots
26. Competitor of Capitol and Epic
29. MIT or NYU
31. Seoul's home
32. Painter Picasso
36. Nervous twitch
38. Congregation leader
39. Invites
42. Modifying wd.
44. AP rival
45. Brownish
46. Impudent back talk
48. Cheer for a torero
49. Finish in front
50. "Don't get any funny ___!"
55. Brooks or Gibson
56. Long-distance number starter
57. Kemo Sabe's companion
58. Concorde, e.g.
59. Phone bk. info
60. Bawl out

DOWN

1. Grand ___ (sporty Pontiacs)
2. Mauna ___ (Hawaiian volcano)
3. ___ of war
4. Fit ___ fiddle
5. Part of R&R
6. Game show host
7. Cleans the blackboard
8. Sass
9. Sir ___ Newton
10. "Rise and ___!"
11. The ___ and the Papas
19. One ___ kind
21. Mighty tree
22. To's opposite
23. Tree with needles
25. "Got it!" cries
27. Studio stages
28. Mai ___ (drink)
30. Apr. 15th advisor
33. Heat meas.
34. Cut (off)
35. You ___ (one of us)

Puzzle 80

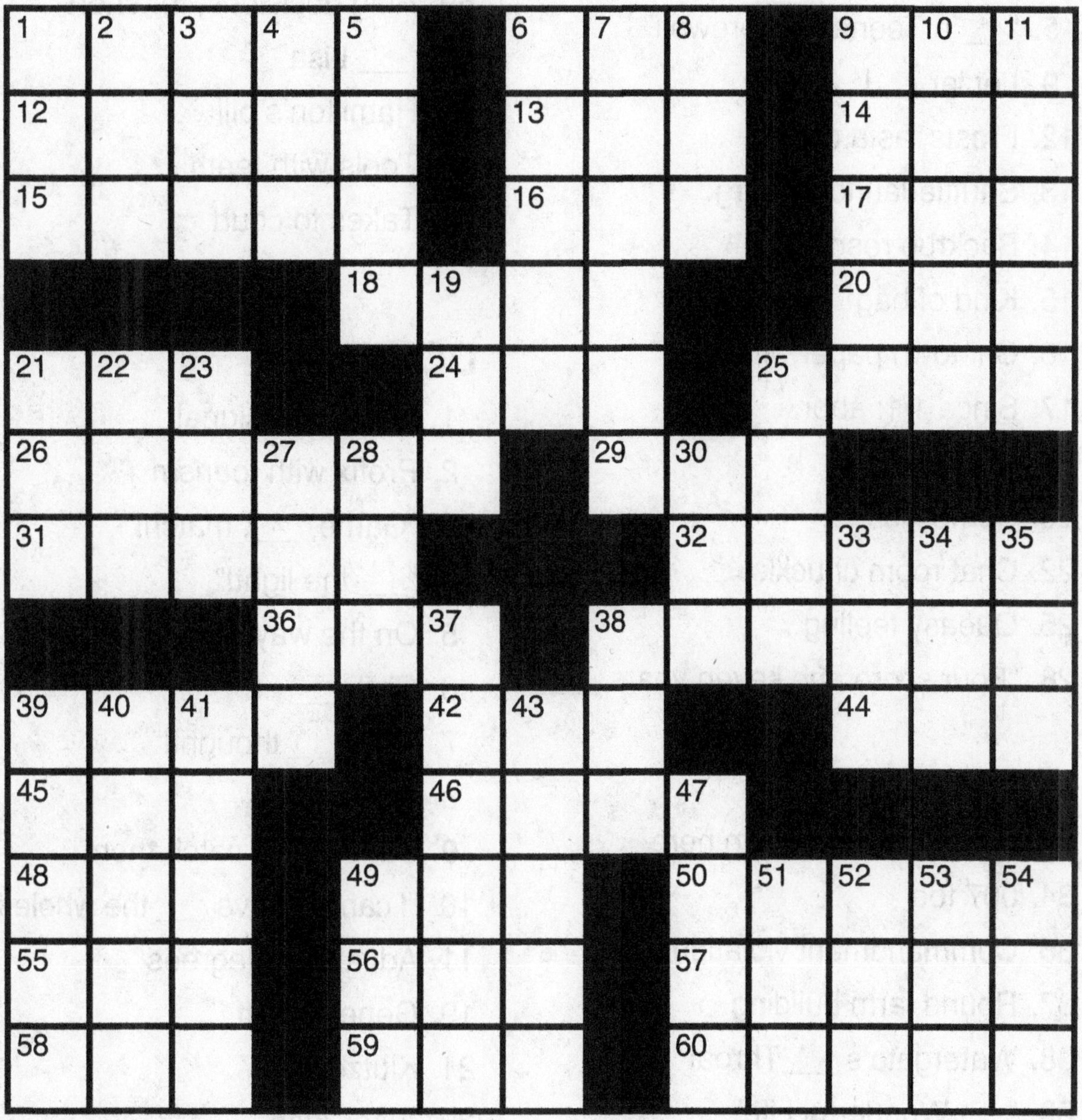

37. Vegas attraction
38. Slumber party garb
39. Parts of molecules
40. Red-tag events
41. Prepared to pray
43. Copenhageners, e.g.
47. Takes a chair
49. Was victorious
51. Med. school grad
52. Rocker Brian
53. U.S./Eur. divider
54. Instant lawn

Solution on Page 319

ACROSS

1. Lucy's partner
5. "___ a Teenage Werewolf"
9. Let 'er ___!
12. Frosts, as a cake
13. Shuttle-launching org.
14. Backrub response
15. Kind of bag
16. Chi-town paper, with "the"
17. Since 1/1: abbr.
18. Goof up
20. Comes in last
22. Chat room chuckle
25. Queasy feeling
28. "Four score and seven years ___
. . ."
29. Green Gables girl
30. People rush to get in here
34. 007 foe
36. Commandment violation
37. Round farm building
38. Watergate's ___ Throat
39. "___ Wonderful Life"
41. Moon lander, for short
42. Hold in high regard
44. PC application file extension
45. With dispatch
48. Basic cleaner
50. Louisville Slugger
51. "___ closed!"

54. Committed perjury
58. Numero ___
59. Ring decisions, for short
60. "___ Lisa"
61. Hamilton's bill
62. Tools with teeth
63. Takes to court

DOWN

1. Telegraph signal
2. Prefix with tourism
3. "Game, ___, match!"
4. "___ the light!"
5. On the way
6. Civil ___
7. "Just ___ thought!"
8. Valuable fur
9. Sunbathers catch them
10. "I can't believe ___ the whole thing!"
11. Advanced degrees
19. Genetic stuff
21. Klutzes
22. Actor Alan
23. Shrek, for one
24. Word before Ranger or Wolf
26. Join forces
27. Lacking meaning
31. Tick off
32. The "A" in A-Rod
33. "Sock it ___!"

35. Intl. oil group
40. TV's "Judging ___"
43. Religious factions
45. Be adjacent to
46. Window glass
47. "This must weigh ___!"
49. They line some old streets

52. Alias initials
53. Female pig
55. Letters of debt
56. Reverse of WSW
57. "___ Rheingold"

Solution on Page 320

ACROSS

1. Southwest Indian
5. TV hosts
8. Sorrowful sound
12. ___ the Terrible
13. Nasdaq debut: abbr.
14. Duo plus one
15. Toppled
16. Natural tanner
17. Great review
18. Out of one's mind
20. Makes amends
22. All's fair in it
23. Barbecued treat
24. "What'd you say?"
27. Work at, as a trade
29. The out crowd
33. Barely made, with "out"
35. "Uh-huh!"
37. Trickle out
38. Extend, as a subscription
40. Salty sauce
42. Go by plane
43. Defy a commandment
45. It's perpendicular to long.
47. Lacking pigment
50. Changes, as the Constitution
54. Bring up, as children
55. "Gosh, it's cold!"
57. Ark builder
58. Curly cabbage
59. Luau garland
60. Sandwich fish
61. Cross-country equipment
62. Letters on an ambulance
63. Glitch

DOWN

1. LP player
2. Kitchen hot spot
3. Best buds
4. Acquired relative
5. Scroogelike
6. "Brain" of a PC
7. Submarine detector
8. Flashing lights
9. Persia, now
10. Donate
11. Garden tools
19. 40 winks
21. ___ Lizzie (Model T)
24. "Hannah and ___ Sisters"
25. Guitar cousin
26. Cooped clucker
28. "Absolutely!"
30. Ump
31. NJ neighbor
32. Work under cover
34. Longs for
36. North Star

39. Triumph

41. Thanksgiving tuber

44. Barnes & ____

46. Camp shelters

47. Vessels like Noah's

48. Plumber's concern

49. ____ Ha'i ("South Pacific" song)

51. Verb accompanier

52. Delany of "China Beach"

53. Kind of carpet

56. Radiation unit

Solution on Page 320

ACROSS

1. A lot
5. Bean counter, for short
8. Co. honchos
12. Restaurant chain acronym
13. Fedora or fez
14. ___ Romeo (sports car)
15. Ritzy
16. Crumb carrier
17. Separate, as flour or ashes
18. Some linens
20. Horned animal
22. Italian cheese
24. Bashful
27. Threaded fastener
30. Map lines: abbr.
31. Restroom, informally
32. Catches red-handed
33. McMahon and Sullivan
34. Stubborn animal
35. Mentalist Geller
36. Con's opposite
37. Some noblemen
38. Undergrad degs.
39. Depart's opposite
41. State west of Mont.
42. Make potable, as sea water
46. Slender
49. Driving range peg
51. "___ she blows!"

52. Corner piece in chess
53. Songwriter Gershwin
54. "___ Lama Ding Dong" (1961 hit)
55. Hankerings
56. Lo-___: lite
57. Abide by

DOWN

1. Restaurant valet's income
2. "Oops!"
3. Bloodhound's asset
4. Globes
5. Gorge
6. ___-Hellenic (like the ancient Olympics)
7. Waits upon
8. Wine barrel
9. Pharmaceutical giant ___ Lilly
10. "Ferris Bueller's Day ___"
11. Took a load off
19. Pull along
21. ___ Altos, Calif.
23. Passion
24. Nasty remark
25. ___ of Fame
26. Designer St. Laurent
27. Rebuff
28. Actress Irene of "Fame"
29. Score-producing stats
33. Inconsistent

176

1	2	3	4		5	6	7		8	9	10	11
12					13				14			
15					16				17			
18				19			20	21				
			22			23				24	25	26
27	28	29				30				31		
32					33				34			
35				36				37				
38				39			40					
			41				42			43	44	45
46	47	48			49	50			51			
52					53				54			
55					56				57			

34. Eminent conductor

36. Rocket launch site

37. Eden woman

40. Perfect

41. Printers' needs

43. Melville captain

44. ___ duck

45. Cafeteria carrier

46. Hear, as a case

47. Groundbreaking tool

48. Elementary particle

50. Historical period

Solution on Page 320

ACROSS

1. ___ but true
4. Pt. of speech
7. "Like, no way!"
11. Ask too many questions
12. Study feverishly
14. Nightclub in a Manilow song
15. Fee, ___, foe, fum
16. "___ honest with you . . ."
17. Owl sound
18. Sink outlet
20. Revise
22. Baseball's DiMaggio
23. Defective firecracker
24. Madison Avenue worker
27. Comic DeLuise
28. Wet dirt
31. Impoverished
32. Sty mother
33. ___ stick
34. Alternatives to Macs
35. "___, humbug!"
36. Island welcome
37. "___ Tin Tin"
38. Homophone for new
39. Beaded calculators
41. Mr. Spock's forte
44. Worry
45. Spicy Asian cuisine
47. Tic-toe connection

49. "Stop right there!"
50. Kitten's plaything
51. Short Red Cross course?
52. Skillfully
53. Was introduced to
54. "You there!"

DOWN

1. Coppertone no.
2. Like a dust bowl
3. One who tints fabrics
4. Film director's cry
5. Pilotless plane
6. Poke
7. Was in pain
8. Shortly
9. Apple MP3 player
10. Jack Sprat's bane
13. Pasture
19. Slightly open
21. Britain's Queen ___
24. Computer program, for short
25. Holliday of the Old West
26. Hip-hop's ___ Def
27. Cry from Homer Simpson
28. Cow comment
29. "That's disgusting!"
30. ER pronouncement
32. Soundness of mind
33. Outlet insert

178

35. Pen name

36. Consecrate with oil

37. Falling apart at the seams

38. Harsh reflection

39. Spirited horse

40. Boxer's cue

42. Something to scratch

43. Part of a Dracula costume

44. Loan org.

46. Lunch meat

48. Weep

Solution on Page 320

ACROSS

1. Butterfingers' cry
5. ___ "Howdy Doody" time!
8. Baseball hats
12. Takes advantage of
13. Corp. boss
14. ___ Krishna
15. Talon
16. Shrouded in mystery
18. Not vert.
19. Page or LaBelle
20. Evening hrs.
21. Pre-calc course
23. Chop
25. Gomer Pyle was one
27. Fit for consumption
31. Newspaper page
32. Votes against
33. Goes over the limit
36. Dad's brothers
38. Go to waste
39. Coward of the stage
40. "___ will be done"
43. Legitimate
45. Alehouse
48. Poster paints
50. Love's antithesis
51. SeaWorld attraction
52. "Citizen Kane" studio
53. U.K. native
54. Appeal to God
55. Japanese currency
56. State with a panhandle: abbr.

DOWN

1. Toe stubber's cry
2. Scandinavian capital
3. Partridge's perch, in song
4. Away from NNE
5. Frigid epoch
6. Midterm or final
7. Relieve
8. Friend of Fidel
9. Seniors' org.
10. Stiffly neat
11. "Be with you in a coupla ___"
17. Like a 4–4 score
19. Sewing basket item
22. Passenger
24. Flinch
25. Rapper ___ Def
26. iPhone download
28. Pro slugger's workplace
29. Caustic chemical
30. Road curve
34. Winged peace symbol
35. Like the night sky
36. A choir may sing in it
37. Doze (off)
40. 'Vette roof option

41. German mister
42. Community gym site
44. Great Salt ___
46. Power co.
47. Phi ___ Kappa
49. Take care of a bill
50. "Entourage" network

Solution on Page 321

ACROSS

1. More than -er
4. Smidgen
7. End-of-the-week cry
11. Notwithstanding that, briefly
12. Common filename extension
13. Hitchcock's "___ Window"
14. Steamy
15. Like Jack Sprat's diet
17. Military organization
18. Artfully escape
20. "Just the facts, ___"
22. On again, as a lantern
23. Shoe part
27. In an uncluttered way
30. World Wide ___
31. Crooner Perry
34. Beaver's exclamation
35. Gives under pressure
36. "How was ___ know?"
37. Bicycle for two
39. Houston nine
41. Beverly Hills's ___ Drive
45. "Piece of cake!"
47. FBI operative
48. Run away
51. Charged particles
53. Barracks bed
54. Ringer
55. Female deer
56. Drink with a head on it
57. Squid squirts
58. Build (on)
59. Remote

DOWN

1. Bygone anesthetic
2. Push roughly
3. Sum
4. Wipe out electronically
5. Logger's tool
6. "___ me up, Scotty"
7. Aerial railway cars
8. Switz. neighbor
9. "___ Woman" (Reddy song)
10. Cook in hot oil
16. Caught in the act
19. Flintstones pet
21. "___ day now . . ."
24. Bygone airline
25. Brain wave readout, for short
26. "Sesame Street" network
28. Andre of tennis
29. First-down yardage
31. Org. in Tom Clancy books
32. Extra NBA periods
33. Bon ___ (witty remark)
35. Urban air problem
37. Up ___ point
38. Rubbed out

40. Film vault collection

42. Coffee that won't keep you up

43. ___ Gay (WWII plane)

44. Playful aquatic animal

46. "Star Wars" sage

48. Crime-fighting org.

49. NFL Hall-of-Famer Dawson

50. BPOE member

52. Silent assent

Solution on Page 321

ACROSS

1. Open ___ night
4. Ending with cash or bombard
7. So-so marks
11. Sort of: suff.
12. "Let's Get It On" singer
14. Gomorrah gala
15. Death Valley is below it
17. Schoenberg opera "Moses und ___"
18. 100-member group
19. Cavity filler: abbr.
21. "My Country, ___ of Thee"
22. ___-or situation
26. Respond to a stimulus
29. Dander
30. ___ Lilly and Company
31. Great Salt Lake's state
32. Household sets
33. Repose
34. Advanced degree
35. Antagonist
36. Confused fight
37. Mortarboard attachment
39. Tic-___-toe
40. Female in a flock
41. Prophet at Delphi
45. Cat or engine sound
48. Poverty-stricken
50. "___ I care!"
51. Courtroom pledge
52. Hyundai rival
53. Henpecks
54. "Give ___ break!"
55. Double curve

DOWN

1. Young lady
2. Words of understanding
3. Detective Charlie
4. "Aha!"
5. Roof overhangs
6. Loaf with seeds
7. Seashore
8. Blunder
9. Swelled head
10. Roget wd.
13. Church officials
16. Door fastener
20. Six-sided game piece
23. Dog command
24. ". . . or ___! (threat)"
25. Baptism, for one
26. Litter's littlest
27. Kett of old comics
28. Satisfied sounds
29. "Now ___ seen everything!"
32. Holy Ohio city?
33. Summary
35. ___ and far between

36. Mrs. Washington
38. Feudal workers
39. Rich pastry
42. Pepsi rival
43. Lane of "Superman"
44. Chapters in history
45. Pot's partner

46. Made in the ___
47. Eighteen-wheeler
49. The Beatles' "___ the Walrus"

Solution on Page 321

ACROSS

1. English TV-radio inits.
4. They're exchanged at the altar
8. Cut the grass
11. Actor Neeson
13. "I ___, I saw, I conquered"
14. "That's disgusting!"
15. ___ point (never)
16. Abbr. on a contour map
17. Foxlike
18. Valentine symbol
20. Some are bitter or sworn
22. Stag or doe
24. "SNL" network
25. Cleanup hitter's stat
27. NASDAQ competitor
30. Sounds of pleasure
33. Unimpressive brain size
34. Spills the beans
36. Was ahead
37. "The Magic Mountain" author
39. Terra firma
40. Tai ___ (exercise method)
41. Bellhop's burden
43. "To ___ his own"
45. Mobile home?
49. Bakers get a rise out of it
52. Twitch
53. Pack (down)
55. "Loose ___ sink ships"
56. Yoko of music
57. "Tickle me" doll
58. Ballroom blunder
59. Buddhist sect
60. Store (away)
61. Avenue crossers: abbr.

DOWN

1. Washed-out feeling
2. Munch
3. Pizza topping
4. Skating surface
5. Roy's cowgirl partner
6. Prophetic sign
7. Deadly sins number
8. Kids' party game
9. Leer at
10. Reasons
12. The ___ the merrier!
19. Camper's shelter
21. Wharton deg.
23. Some whiskeys
25. Tach. letters
26. "Luck ___ Lady Tonight"
28. ___-mo camera
29. Peace Nobelist Wiesel
31. Half a laugh
32. Reagan-era mil. program

35. Murder

38. Catch in the act

42. Bill of Microsoft

44. Irish native

45. From ___: completely

46. Queue

47. Soda fountain treat

48. Bullets and such

50. Roasting rod

51. Cough syrup amts.

54. "Right in the kisser!" preceder

Solution on Page 321

ACROSS

1. Yup's opposite
4. Poet's planet
7. House, in Havana
11. Suffix like -like
12. The Beach Boys' "___ Vibrations"
14. Heads ___, tails you lose
15. "Love ___ neighbor . . ."
16. Companionless
17. Pleased
18. Solar ___
20. Liquid part of blood
22. Mins. add up to them
23. Lungful
24. Lug
27. Capote, familiarly
28. Omaha's state: abbr.
31. Sacred
32. Belly
33. "Ali ___ and the 40 Thieves"
34. It's scanned at checkout: abbr.
35. Peat source
36. "Dear" advice-giver
37. Farrow of "Broadway Danny Rose"
38. Intl. clock standard
40. "Little Women" writer
43. Spoke roughly
47. Cry from Santa
48. Checked out
50. Part of a GI's address

51. ". . . happily ___ after"
52. "___ Peach" (Allman Brothers album)
53. Playing card spot
54. A ___ pittance
55. Candied veggie
56. ___ Ventura (Jim Carrey role)

DOWN

1. Louse eggs
2. Like arson evidence
3. Explanations
4. Girl watcher, perhaps
5. Hotel offerings
6. ___ mot (witticism)
7. Close, but no ___
8. Shoemaker's tools
9. "The King and I" setting
10. Time ___ half
13. Leave
19. "If ___ only knew!"
21. Actress Lucy
24. Fri. preceder
25. Alley ___
26. Doting letters
27. Pull
28. Seize
29. Kind of tide
30. ___ City Rollers
32. Pointed beard

188

33. Flying mammals

35. Took the bait

37. Mary Tyler ___

38. Miss Garbo

39. Lady's title

40. "Um, excuse me"

41. Zero, in tennis

42. Sonny's partner, once

44. Father

45. Ben-Hur, for one

46. Simpleton

49. Hurrah!

Solution on Page 322

ACROSS

1. Detroit labor org.
4. Actress Gardner
7. Jr. high, e.g.
10. Snooty person
12. Rand McNally product
13. The Clintons' alma mater
14. Mano-a-mano
16. Nose tickler
17. Crosses (out)
18. Napped leather
19. Followed a curved path
22. Active person
24. "All in the Family" producer Norman
25. Overage
28. Bed-and-breakfasts
29. China's ___ Tse-tung
30. Locale
32. Iran's capital
34. Exam given face-to-face
35. The triple in a triple play
36. Pizzeria fixtures
37. Security feature
40. Type of test on "CSI"
41. Second to none
42. :-) or :-(
47. Sounds of displeasure
48. Dads
49. ___ bene
50. Plaything
51. Pirate's assent
52. Agt.'s take

DOWN

1. GI entertainers
2. Raggedy doll
3. Grief
4. Famous cookie guy
5. Moving truck
6. Animal that beats its chest
7. "The Sweetest Taboo" singer
8. Clumsy one
9. ___ and now
11. Alternative to briefs
13. 1972 Carly Simon hit
15. Beatty of film
18. Wall St. watchdog
19. Rope-a-dope boxer
20. Lease
21. Chaplin prop
22. University officials
23. Tic-tac-toe loser
26. Father
27. Ollie's partner in comedy
29. It might say WELCOME
31. Golf pro Ernie
33. Bacardi, e.g.

190

36. Ottawa's prov.

37. Adjoin

38. Plastic building block

39. Like a fireplace floor

40. Amount of medicine

42. Eco-friendly org.

43. Indy 500 month

44. ___ a plea

45. Needing no prescription: abbr.

46. ___ King Cole

Solution on Page 322

ACROSS

1. Water closet, informally
4. "Some Like It ___"
7. Edge
10. Put one's hands together
12. Bed-in participant with Lennon
13. Mislay
14. Boxer Oscar ___ Hoya
15. Long. crosser
16. Working hard
17. Revolutionist Guevara
19. Juicy steak
20. Small part played by a big name
23. "Get lost, fly!"
25. Chicago airport
26. Pageant crowns
29. Step to the plate
30. Club ___ (resort chain)
31. Drink slowly
33. ___ Babies
36. Wash away, as soil
38. Lower-left key on many keyboards
39. Inmate who's never getting out
40. Nod's verbal equivalent
43. Letters between "K" and "O"
44. Make the acquaintance of
45. Genetic info transmitter
47. Scott who sued for his freedom
51. Ballerina's bend
52. Traveler's stopover
53. Mentally fit
54. Popular camera type, for short
55. Sleeping spot
56. Ernie Els org.

DOWN

1. Watch display, for short
2. October brew
3. Kilmer of "The Doors"
4. Golf target
5. "Put ___ Happy Face"
6. Rug rat
7. Prefix with tiller
8. Love ___ the air
9. Dole (out)
11. Indiana basketballer
13. Workers, collectively
18. Tiller's tool
19. Suit ___ tee
20. Kernel holder
21. Moby Dick chaser
22. Spouse
23. Stainless metal
24. Stayed out of sight
27. Beginning on
28. "West ___ Story"
30. Old space station
32. Price ___ pound
34. Less than 90 degrees
35. Final degree?

36. "A Nightmare on ___ Street"
37. Orange covers
40. Strike callers
41. Hades
42. ___ to the throne
43. Come to shore
45. Adam's spare part

46. SSW's reverse
48. Grammy category
49. London's locale: abbr.
50. Narc.'s grp.

Solution on Page 322

ACROSS

1. Narc.'s agcy.
4. Disneyland's Enchanted ___ Room
8. Potato, informally
12. Leatherworker's tool
13. Understood, hippie-style
14. Tilting-tower town
15. Chic, to Austin Powers
16. "The ___ Ranger"
17. Risque
18. Glide on the ice
20. Howard Hughes's airline
22. Speed skater Heiden
25. Protestant work ___
29. Once ___ a time . . .
32. Place for eggs
34. Thurman of film
35. ___ to help
36. Andy Capp's wife
37. Hoof sound
38. "Beavis and Butt-Head" laugh
39. Soft drink nut
40. Erie or Huron
41. ___ Arabia
43. Gumbo ingredient
45. Travel rtes.
47. Entirely
51. Hoopla
54. "Haven't ___ you somewhere before?"
57. Fan's rebuke
58. Morays, e.g.
59. Not tied down
60. Barbell abbr.
61. ___ and Means Committee
62. Head-shakers' syllables
63. Agreeable reply

DOWN

1. Beavers' creations
2. Furry "Star Wars" creature
3. "M*A*S*H" star Alan
4. Bathroom floor installer
5. Bachelor's last words
6. Family
7. "This is the thanks ___?"
8. Jack of nursery rhyme
9. Actress Zadora
10. L.A. school
11. "Our ___ Will Come"
19. Take care of
21. ___ behind the ears
23. Data
24. Yo-Yo Ma's instrument
26. Luau dance
27. "Don't worry about me!"
28. Superman accessory
29. Cries of aversion
30. Bit of begging
31. Honolulu's island
33. Relax in the tub

Puzzle 92

37. Group with a common ancestor

39. Tease playfully

42. Attire

44. Religious ceremonies

46. Refine, as flour

48. With proficiency

49. Earring's place

50. At a ___ for words

51. Cut down

52. Pro vote

53. Layer

55. "And here's to you, ___ Robinson . . ."

56. Mouse spotter's cry

Solution on Page 322

ACROSS

1. Garden insect
6. Not outgoing
9. "___ la la" (singing syllables)
12. Nifty, in the '50s
13. Tiny bit
14. Scatter, as seed
15. Courtroom event
16. TV interruptions
17. Spring mo.
18. Dryer buildup
20. Birds of ___
21. "To ___, with Love"
24. Southwestern home material
26. Infamous Amin
27. Mil. officers
28. Marsh plants
32. Tenant
34. Angry outburst
35. Frost's "The Road Not ___"
36. "You're it!" game
37. Like sushi
38. Defeated one
40. Opposite of ant.
41. Like most NBA players
44. Milliner's supply
46. Post-op area
47. Surgery sites, for short
48. Shish ___
53. Brooks of comedy

54. Middling mark
55. Ice house
56. College website suffix
57. NFL six-pointers
58. Ditto!

DOWN

1. Aardvark's morsel
2. The "p" in rpm
3. "Bali ___" ("South Pacific" song)
4. "Make ___ double!"
5. Barbie, for one
6. Prepares for the anthem
7. "If I ___ do it all over again . . ."
8. Football gains: abbr.
9. Ivan the Terrible, e.g.
10. Lariat material
11. Out of kilter
19. ". . . can't believe ___ the whole thing"
20. Jury member
21. Riverbed deposit
22. It's just a thought
23. Insurer's exposure
25. Naval lockup
27. Letterman rival
29. "I'm all ___"
30. Invasion date
31. Mended
33. Auction off

34. Pucker-producing
36. Makes fun of
39. Rip up
41. Newsweek rival
42. Got a perfect score on
43. Doozie
45. Read cursorily

47. World Series mo.
49. Grow older
50. Sandwich on toast
51. Hugs, symbolically
52. Hiss accompanier

Solution on Page 323

ACROSS

1. Maple syrup source
4. Managed care gps.
8. Kind of trip for the conceited
11. "It's a Sin to Tell ___"
13. Roof overhang
14. 1968 hit "Harper Valley ___"
15. Swiss painter Paul
16. Had misgivings about
17. Realtor's unit
18. Makes, as a salary
20. Hurrying
22. Shade of blue
24. "The world will little note, ___ long remember, what we say here": Lincoln
25. Put into service
27. Understands
30. Satellite signal receiver
33. LAPD alert
34. Throat ailment
36. "Man, it's cold!"
37. Suffix with hard or soft
39. "___ Smile" (1976 Hall & Oates hit)
40. Start of some aircraft carriers
41. Some chants
43. AC measures
45. It's her party
49. Astonishes
52. Cozy lodging
53. Pub quaffs
55. Ruler unit
56. Pod occupant
57. Table supports
58. Hawaiian feast
59. One of a deadly septet
60. Sultan of ___ (Babe Ruth)
61. Isle of ___

DOWN

1. Rice wine
2. "It was ___ mistake!"
3. Remington Steele portrayer
4. "On ___ Majesty's Secret Service"
5. Hawaii's second-largest island
6. Pizzeria fixture
7. Alternative to a station wagon or convertible
8. Phrase on the back of a buck
9. Classic muscle cars
10. Inauguration declaration
12. "___, meeny, miney, mo"
19. Back talk
21. Serling of "The Twilight Zone"
23. Butterfly catchers
25. Motor City labor org.
26. Health resort
28. Time in history
29. Belgrade native
31. AARP members

32. 60-min. units

35. ___ down (frisks)

38. CPR expert

42. Arctic barkers

44. Electric or water co.

45. Places for holsters

46. "That's ___ haven't heard"

47. Did away with, as a dragon

48. Dreamcast game company

50. March Madness org.

51. Give the cold shoulder

54. Mach+ jet

Solution on Page 323

ACROSS

1. "Quiet down!"
4. Tracks in mud
8. The "Land of ___"
11. Travels
13. Bushy hairstyle
14. "Where did ___ wrong?"
15. Spring event
16. Put one over on
17. ___-Magnon man
18. Fountain drinks
20. Athletic shoe
22. Singletons
24. Opposite of NNW
25. VH1 rival
27. Outback birds
30. Swiss artist Paul
33. "___ Maria"
34. Boxing ring boundaries
36. ___ Arbor, Mich.
37. Golfing vehicle
39. "Thank Heaven for Little Girls" musical
40. Turkey mo.
41. Meat with eggs
43. Matured
45. Hi-fis
49. Consumerist Ralph
52. Knock the socks off of
53. "It's us against ___"
55. Floor covering
56. ___ Gerard (Buck Rogers portrayer)
57. Against
58. "You said it!"
59. Question's opposite: abbr.
60. Missing
61. CPR expert

DOWN

1. Bilko and Pepper: abbr.
2. Syllables from Santa
3. One way to fall in love
4. Brit. flyboys
5. Tabloid fliers
6. 1982 Disney film starring Jeff Bridges
7. Shoe bottoms
8. Trivial
9. Fairy tale villain
10. Place for a peephole
12. Graceful bird
19. Palm reader, e.g.
21. "___ me if I care"
23. Target of clean air laws
25. Comedian Bernie
26. Flood control proj.
28. AP competitor
29. Big name in computer games
31. Ambient music pioneer Brian

32. Ltr. carrier

35. Aries or Libra

38. Cigarette substance

42. "Heavy" music genre

44. "I could ___ horse!"

45. Sweeping story

46. Minnesota ballplayer

47. "This can't be!"

48. Complete collections

50. Kind of sch.

51. Landlord's check

54. Cambridge sch.

Solution on Page 323

ACROSS

1. Fail to mention
5. Chew the fat
9. Digital readout, for short
12. Prefix with legal or chute
13. Children's head pests
14. Debt acknowledgment
15. Kind of torch on "Survivor"
16. Tetra, doubled
17. "What, me worry?" magazine
18. Tony Blair and others, briefly
20. Drug that dulls the brain
22. Hold back
25. Reel partner
26. Partner of cease
27. Got to one's feet
30. Give ___ shot
31. Barnyard clucker
33. Sticks around
37. "60 Minutes" pundit Andy
40. Like a fiddle
41. "The Continent"
42. A, B, or C
45. Gas additive brand
46. Wall climber
47. Liberals, with "the"
49. Rocklike
53. End-of-summer mo.
54. Truth or ___ (slumber party game)
55. Ripening agent
56. Mahmoud Abbas's grp.
57. Lose traction
58. Lymph bump

DOWN

1. Quit, with "out"
2. ___ tai
3. Get on one's nerves
4. Taiwan's capital
5. Skeleton's place?
6. Hawaiian Punch alternative
7. Cast members
8. ___ Dome (Harding administration scandal)
9. Peru's capital
10. ___ of arms
11. Kind of ranch
19. RNs' coworkers
21. "If ___ say so myself"
22. Mean Amin
23. 2000 "Subway Series" losers
24. HS junior's exam
28. Speed skater Apolo Anton ___
29. ___ blue sea
32. "Bill ___ the Science Guy"
34. Astern
35. Gives in
36. Run of luck

Solution on Page 302

37. Took a breather
38. Publicly gay
39. Parentless child
42. Speech impediment
43. First name in stunts
44. Proofreader's find

48. Part of TGIF: abbr.
50. In times past
51. Stop sign color
52. Dr. with several Grammys

Solution on Page 323

ACROSS

1. Buffet meal carrier
5. "No ifs, ___, or buts!"
9. Cyber guffaw
12. Tex. neighbor
13. Encounter
14. Climbing vine
15. Sound of distress
16. Ill temper
17. Middle grade
18. Ceramist's oven
20. Lascivious looks
22. Globe or ball
25. Cold and ___ season
26. Attempts
27. Bits of wisdom?
30. ___ capita
31. "___ do you do?"
32. Dream letters
34. Shut tight
37. Take as one's own
39. Set down
40. Perfumes
41. Wood strips
44. Abbr. before a name on an envelope
45. Moray, e.g.
46. Adventure story
48. Overwhelmed
52. Treasure hunter's aid
53. "___ out?" (dealer's query)
54. "Mona ___"
55. Conditions
56. Tech sch. grad
57. Line-___ veto

DOWN

1. Mix or Cruise
2. "King Kong" studio
3. Chicken ___ king
4. Union member
5. Mosey along
6. Opposite of "Ja"
7. ___ Monte (food giant)
8. "A Streetcar Named Desire" woman
9. Dog pests
10. Finished
11. Soapmaking substances
19. E-file receiver
21. Afr. neighbor
22. Oil treatment letters
23. Veep's superior
24. Add to the staff
25. Not a lot
27. Pea holder
28. Author Hubbard
29. Aug. follower
31. The Say ___ Kid (Willie Mays)
33. Shasta and Olympus, for short
35. PC key near Ctrl

Puzzle 97

36. TV collie
37. "___ your age!"
38. National park in Alaska
40. Ringo on drums
41. Big hauler
42. Fall faller
43. European mountains
44. Wide-eyed
47. Political commentator Coulter
49. Twain's talent
50. U-turn from WNW
51. Hydroelectric project

Solution on Page 324

ACROSS

1. UCLA rival
4. Declare openly
8. Cow poke?
12. Sony rival
13. Doily material
14. Radiant glow
15. Persona ___ grata
16. Shredded
18. It may be wood-burning
20. "Dedicated to the ___ Love"
21. Yearn (for)
23. Romantic recitals
27. Flower support
29. Old King of rhyme
32. "That feels so-o-o good!"
33. "Am ___ time?"
34. Number of little pigs or blind mice
35. Sr.'s test
36. Calendar abbr.
37. Jellystone Park denizen
38. Appealed earnestly
39. Swashbuckling Flynn
41. Result of over-exercising
43. Allows
46. Very skilled
49. First-rate
53. "___, though I walk through the valley . . ."
54. Inactive
55. Playbill listing
56. Subj. for immigrants
57. Unskilled laborer
58. Hunt and peck
59. Fawn's mother

DOWN

1. Ash containers
2. Aberdeen native
3. Kitchen gadget that turns
4. From another planet
5. Panel truck
6. Word form for "eight"
7. Remove from a mother's milk
8. Place for a barbecue
9. Regret
10. Bruin Bobby
11. Prosecutors, briefly
17. Sioux shelter
19. Get-up-and-go
22. Rebounding sound
24. Keen of sight
25. Mature filly
26. Cast off
27. Builder's area
28. Sightseeing trip
30. Nonprofit website suffix
31. Luke Skywalker's sister
34. "Tippecanoe and ___ too"
38. High degree

40. Ancient

42. À la ___ (one way to order)

44. Diplomat's asset

45. Move in the breeze

47. Mexican moolah

48. It's tall when exaggerated

49. Part of an iceberg that's visible

50. "___ to Billy Joe"

51. Arafat's grp.

52. Mind reading, for short

Solution on Page 324

ACROSS

1. Popular sneakers
5. Rambler mfr.
8. Charged atoms
12. Sarcastic agreement
13. Scientist's milieu
14. Picked from the stack of cards
15. Etc., for one
16. Old vinyl
17. "Gone with the Wind" estate
18. Mall units
20. Oodles
21. "L.A. Law" co-star Susan
22. Implore
24. Twin Mary-Kate or Ashley
27. Buck Rogers player Gerard
28. Boob tubes
31. London lavatory
32. Slip through the clutches of
34. Stir-fry pan
35. Firecracker that fizzles
36. "___ a life!"
37. String quartet member
39. Proverbial sword-beater
40. Where to hang one's hat
41. Nick at ___
44. Instruction book
47. Book after II Chronicles
48. Pro and ___
49. Out of control

51. Sixty minutes
52. Camp bed
53. Wall St. inits.
54. Middle of March
55. Savings acct. alternatives
56. Part of NAACP: abbr.

DOWN

1. Seoul-based automaker
2. Declines
3. Borrower's burden
4. Walked with a purpose
5. Back street
6. Atlas contents
7. Network with an eye logo
8. Luggage attachment
9. Taken by mouth
10. Roman "fiddler"
11. Swing at a fly
19. Go back on one's word
22. Auction offer
23. 7-___
24. Up there in years
25. Comic Costello
26. Lawn makeup
27. ___ reaction
28. Duet number
29. Encyclopedia bk.
30. Precursor of reggae
33. Novelist Deighton

38. Big lizard
39. Bosc and Bartlett
40. Trousers
41. Classic soda brand
42. Polo Ralph Lauren competitor
43. "T" on a test
44. Frame of mind

45. Grant and Carter
46. Defeat
48. XXX times X
50. Author Kesey

Solution on Page 324

ACROSS

1. Naturalist John
5. Special ___: military force
8. Tire-pressure letters
11. Mr. Peanut prop
12. This is ___ toy
14. Tire filler
15. Hit, as a fly
16. Kennedy and Turner
17. Printer's need
18. Gomorrah's sister city
20. Musical sounds
22. "___ Jacques" (children's song)
24. Biblical boat
25. Uncles' mates
26. Hangmen's ropes
29. ER workers
30. Chinese frying pan
31. Some Caribbean music
33. Teeter-totter
36. Language of ancient Rome
38. "The Karate ___" (1984)
39. Revises, as text
40. More secure
43. Fulton's power
45. Billiard stick
46. World's fair
48. Chums
51. Paintings and such
52. Playwright Simon
53. Car roof with removable panels
54. West of old films
55. Lorne Michaels's show
56. "To thine own ___ be true"

DOWN

1. Roast hosts, briefly
2. Negotiator with GM
3. Looking at it one way
4. Sharp comeback
5. Not fooled by
6. Limerick, e.g.
7. Pt. of EST
8. Ache
9. Trig ratio
10. Really gets to
13. The Jetsons' dog
19. ___ Plaines, IL
21. Gives the green light
22. Distant
23. Seeks office
24. Thumbs up
26. "This instant!"
27. Pre-repair job figure
28. Funny sketch
30. Roll of dough
32. The "A" of Q&A: abbr.
34. Scratch (out), as a living

35. Ambulance sound
36. Civil War general
37. Changes to fit
40. Pyramid scheme, e.g.
41. Saintly radiance
42. Gala gathering

43. Whirl
44. Turnpike charge
47. Ballot marks
49. Online guffaw
50. Tanning lotion abbr.

Solution on Page 324

ACROSS

1. "Killer" PC program
4. Hug givers
8. Scatters, as seed
12. Sandra of "Gidget"
13. Sugar source
14. Came to rest on a wire, e.g.
15. Light switch positions
16. Shave-haircut link
17. "All ___ are off!"
18. Cries convulsively
20. Golly!
22. Guide
25. Saudis and Iraqis
29. That makes ___ of sense
32. Fisherman's bucketful
34. Datebook abbr.
35. Availability extremes
38. Picnic scurrier
39. Decomposes
40. Chooses
41. Martini & ___ vermouth
43. Mediocre
45. Pull a scam
47. "Meet Me ___ Louis"
50. Pro or con, in a debate
53. Great server on the court
56. Affirmative response
58. Elvis's middle name
59. Scrabble piece
60. Gun owners' org.
61. Garden entrance
62. Acorn producers
63. Scoundrel

DOWN

1. "Much ___ About Nothing"
2. Ballpoints, e.g.
3. Mexican money
4. Lower in esteem
5. Stimpy's partner
6. ___ school
7. For men only
8. Cavalry sword
9. Cheer for a matador
10. Knack for comebacks
11. Rds. or aves.
19. Deli orders, briefly
21. "Do I dare to ___ peach?"
23. Ending with peek or bug
24. Pub game
26. "Take ___ from me!"
27. Short hit, in baseball
28. Comprehends
29. Way off
30. Carson's successor
31. Feedbag fill
33. "Should that be the case"
36. Peter, Paul and Mary, e.g.
37. Apollo 11 destination

(Crossword grid)

42. Movie division

44. Fathers on a farm

46. Western mil. alliance

48. Lip-___ (not really sing)

49. Trillion: prefix

50. Drop in the middle

51. Later-yrs. nest egg

52. Com preceder

54. Undercover org.

55. Fraternal lodge member

57. Mournful

Solution on Page 325

ACROSS

1. Butt
4. Depletes, as strength
8. "Puppy Love" singer Paul
12. Get from ___ B
13. Gator's cousin
14. Wart causer, in legend
15. Cultural support org.
16. Fairy-tale meanie
17. Manage, as a bar
18. Robert of "Raging Bull"
20. Sounds
22. Fellows
23. And so on, briefly
24. Bushy 'do
27. Joan of ___
28. I. M. ___
31. Pigpen cry
32. Sauté
33. Communicate by hand
34. Sgt.'s superiors
35. Jabber
36. Corporate VIPs
37. "It's c-c-cold!"
38. Railroad stop: abbr.
40. Few and far between
43. Wyoming range
47. Brazilian soccer great
48. Broadcasts
50. "Beavis and Butt-Head" laugh
51. Zoo fixture
52. ___ and polish
53. Call to a calf
54. Not much
55. Spinning toys
56. ___-Caps (candy brand)

DOWN

1. Author Ayn
2. Suit to ___ (fit perfectly)
3. Mournful cry
4. Make points
5. Light bulb gas
6. ___ favor: Sp.
7. Overlook's offering
8. Basement's opposite
9. Turndowns
10. "Citizen ___"
11. Opposite of subtracts
19. Post-accident reassurance
21. Where some stks. trade
24. EarthLink competitor
25. In great shape
26. MD's associates
27. Two-by-two vessel
28. Crusty dessert
29. It may be puffed up
30. Walk-___ (clients without appointments)
32. Orient

214

33. Improvisational singing style

35. 12-mo. periods

37. Kennel club classification

38. Get undressed

39. Midterms, e.g.

40. Pet adoption org.

41. Fuel from a bog

42. Pond organism

44. ___ Law (basic law of current flow)

45. Gas in advertising lights

46. "Scram!"

49. Wall St. debut

Solution on Page 325

ACROSS

1. ___ and away
4. Went down like a stone
8. "___ want for Christmas . . ."
12. Owed
13. Shah's domain, once
14. Urban unrest
15. Chime in
16. Thin coin
17. "Smoke ___ in Your Eyes"
18. Man or Wight
20. Academic URL ender
22. Incantation start
25. Takes five
29. Oh, sure
32. Play parts
34. "___ ol' me?"
35. Store window word
36. When repeated, a ballroom dance
37. Actress Anderson
38. Opposite of SSW
39. Smell horrible
40. Newspaper essayist's page
41. Home of Arizona State
43. Gardener's spring purchase
45. Well put
47. Say no to, as a bill
50. Woes
53. The tops
56. Passports, for example: abbr.

58. ___ as a pin
59. It follows 11
60. Sty resident
61. Johnny-___-lately
62. Drunkards
63. Filming locale

DOWN

1. Medicine-approving org.
2. BMW competitor
3. 1981 Beatty film
4. Lesser-played half of a "45"
5. Bush spokesman Fleischer
6. '60s war site
7. Leg joint
8. Quarrel
9. Tell a whopper
10. Real estate unit
11. ___ in the bag
19. Running behind
21. AMA members
23. Speed contest
24. Partner of pains
26. Sty food
27. Prong
28. Moved on ice
29. "___ It Romantic?"
30. Curse
31. Type of school: abbr.
33. ___ five (rest)
37. Ore deposit

39. Not dem.
42. Kindergarten adhesive
44. ___ the score (gets revenge)
46. Beach shades
48. Gratuities
49. "Garfield" canine
50. Business mag
51. Virgo's predecessor

52. Escape, as from jail
54. Tic-tac-toe win
55. To be or ___ to be
57. Cpl.'s superior

Solution on Page 325

ACROSS

1. "Gomer ___, USMC"
5. Small plateau
9. ___-Cone (summer snack)
12. Ear-busting
13. Followers of the Pied Piper of Hamelin
14. Lend a hand
15. "Cool, man!"
16. Voyage with Captain Kirk
17. Mich. neighbor
18. Let up
20. Christmas tree shedding
22. Exaggerate
24. Tue. preceder
27. Young guy
28. Blubbers
32. Like a phoenix out of the ashes
34. Bring into existence
36. Look at amorously
37. "___ make myself clear?"
38. Election day: abbr.
39. Give, as homework
42. Jock
45. Black-tie affairs
50. Volleyball court divider
51. Betsy or Diana
53. Oom-pah band instrument
54. Krazy ___ of the comics
55. Big furniture retailer
56. Follow orders
57. Concert stage item
58. Took a tumble
59. "Alice" diner

DOWN

1. Ballerina's knee bend
2. Luke Skywalker's mentor
3. San ___ Obispo, Calif.
4. U2 guitarist (with "The")
5. Actor with the catchphrase, "I pity the fool!"
6. Brought in, as a salary
7. Animal in a roundup
8. Inquired
9. Leave port
10. Supreme Court count
11. ___ and ends
19. Loser to Clinton in 1996
21. Prescription quantity
23. Florist's vehicle
24. China's Chairman ___
25. Part of NATO: abbr.
26. Zilch
29. Feedbag grain
30. AC meas.
31. The Who's "I Can ___ for Miles"
33. Flippered mammal
34. Gear tooth
35. Boxing venue

37. Engine type
40. Letter flourish
41. Stir up, as a fire
42. Paul who wrote "My Way"
43. Group of athletes
44. Internet address opener
46. Molecule building block

47. Oil change go-with
48. Brother of Cain
49. Simon ___
52. "I've got a mule, her name is ___"

Solution on Page 325

ACROSS

1. Blacken on the barbecue
5. Letters before an alias
8. Eccentric
11. Wingless parasites
12. Play the ponies
13. Online marketplace
14. Nights before holidays
15. Cereal grass
16. Five-and-___
17. Felt hat
19. Brings together
21. "Well, that's obvious!"
22. Daddies
23. Part of B&B
26. Noticeable opening
28. Snooped (around)
32. ___ about (roughly)
34. ___ culpa (my fault)
36. PBS science program
37. ___ committee
39. Doberman's warning
41. Salary
42. Sheep's cry
44. Spitfire fliers, for short
46. Soak up
49. New Balance competitor
53. Red vegetable
54. Have the deed to
56. Lopsided victory
57. They may be parallel or uneven
58. Cleaning cloth
59. ___ good example
60. Abrade
61. Pooh's middle name?
62. "Iliad" setting

DOWN

1. Musical staff insignia
2. Honey factory
3. Scored 100 percent on
4. Patch the lawn
5. "___, Martin and John"
6. Lock opener
7. Devoured
8. Newspaper notice
9. Notre ___
10. Changes the color of
13. Phonograph inventor
18. Toupee, slangily
20. Indian bread
23. Feathered stole
24. Dead-___ street
25. Play-___ (kids' clay)
27. Wooden pin
29. ___ up (absorb)
30. Actress ___ Marie Saint
31. Calendar square
33. Androids
35. Adapt music for the band

38. Automobile
40. X-ray dose unit
43. Cancel the launch
45. Blue-ribbon position
46. E.g., e.g.
47. Gal's sweetheart
48. Many a Bosnian

50. Active one
51. Garage occupant
52. Don't leave!
55. Baby's bawl

Solution on Page 326

ACROSS

1. Prefix meaning "three"
4. Gore and Sharpton
7. "Little ___ of Horrors"
11. "I've ___ it!"
12. Be a snitch
14. Cadabra preceder
15. Jack's preceder
16. Medal of Honor recipient
17. Disoriented
18. 12th grader
20. "The Simpsons" clerk
22. Not feral
23. Notice
27. ___ out (postponed, in a way)
29. Musical Wonder
30. Scannable mdse. bars
31. Approx. landing hr.
32. "Here's to you!," and others
36. Gazes steadily
39. Daryl Hannah comedy of '84
40. Lofty tennis shots
41. Word before a dropped maiden name
42. Aid
45. It marches on
48. Plenty
50. To the ___ degree
51. "X-Files" subjects
52. At no charge
53. Spy's org.
54. Hue
55. Double-curve letter
56. Suffix with north

DOWN

1. "Get a load of ___!"
2. Leaf-gathering tool
3. Like some twins
4. Where telecommuters work
5. Looked lecherously
6. Camera type, for short
7. Military greeting
8. Premium cable channel
9. Hospital areas: abbr.
10. Butter serving
13. Oodles
19. Bond creator Fleming
21. Household animal
24. From then on
25. Quote as an example
26. Afternoon socials
27. Wheel tracks
28. For each one
33. Most sensible
34. Philosopher Lao-___
35. Bookcase part
36. Candidate lists
37. Coin flips
38. Crunched muscles

43. Use a swizzle stick

44. Larger ___ life

45. King in a Steve Martin song

46. "___ Were a Rich Man"

47. Calendar abbr.

49. Metal to be refined

Solution on Page 326

ACROSS

1. Defeat decisively
5. Tennis do-over
8. Lion's share
12. Ruler division
13. Sedan or coupe
14. Now we're in trouble!
15. Rancor
16. Rap's Dr. ___
17. ___-American relations
18. ___ in the back (betrays)
20. Mexican snacks
22. PC "Go back!" key
24. Tobacco smoke component
25. Unending
29. Salad servers
33. Load for Jack and Jill
34. Took the pennant
36. Heavy burden
37. Comic orphan
39. Creditor's demand
41. Gun owners' grp.
43. Lobbying org.
44. "___ the Ides of March"
47. Argue a case
51. Pepsi, for one
52. ___ been there
54. Waikiki Beach locale
55. Dice throw
56. "Not my error" notation
57. Preowned
58. Baseball's Hershiser
59. "Evil Woman" rock grp.
60. Reps.' foes

DOWN

1. Barbecue entrée
2. "Don't count ___!"
3. USC rival
4. Cold War symbol
5. Type of PC screen
6. Work to get, as someone's trust
7. Trick or ___
8. Nuclear explosion aftermath
9. Dayton's state
10. Mamas' boys
11. Nevertheless
19. Tax ID
21. Tabby
23. Crow sound
25. Govt. air-quality watchdog
26. Light brown
27. Ich Bin ___ Berliner: JFK
28. Slice (off)
30. One-eighty from SSW
31. "Annie Get Your ___"
32. Concorde, notably: abbr.
35. Get a little shuteye
38. Historic period
40. Talk, talk, talk

Puzzle 107

42. Come about
44. Unmannered fellow
45. Vogue competitor
46. Diabolical
48. "___ on Down the Road"
49. Throat-clearing sound
50. Bombs that don't explode
51. Magnon start
53. Green prefix

Solution on Page 326

ACROSS

1. Son ___ gun
4. Pole, e.g.
8. What swish shots miss
12. "___ Are My Sunshine"
13. Vatican VIP
14. Opera highlight
15. Blazed the trail
16. Sports cable channel
17. It may be rolled out in the rain
18. Window ledge
20. "___ Had a Hammer"
22. Friend in war
25. Party givers
29. Arterial blockage
32. Leaning tower city
34. Ascot
35. Become bushed
36. Hair goo
37. Pie à la ___
38. GP's assistants
39. Artist Salvador
40. Fills with wonder
41. Africa's Sierra ___
43. June 6, 1944
45. Hold the title to
47. Eyelid attachment
50. IOU
53. Fail to include
56. Clodhopper
58. Sheet of glass
59. ___-Rooter
60. Rx watchdog
61. Poses questions
62. Rolling stone's lack
63. Bill at the bar

DOWN

1. Popeye's Olive
2. Enemies
3. German auto
4. Compete in a bee
5. Part of UCLA
6. PC program
7. ___, vidi, vici (Caesar's boast)
8. 3:1 or 7:2, e.g.
9. Roth ___
10. Bygone Russian space station
11. Tree liquid
19. Missing a deadline
21. Govt. mortgage provider
23. Org. for Annika Sorenstam
24. Give way
26. Stash away
27. Beach washer
28. Observes
29. Bottom-row PC key
30. Toe the ___ (obey)
31. Approximately
33. Lost control on ice

37. Central American Indian

39. Morning moisture

42. Student's jottings

44. Voices above tenors

46. Cliff's pal on "Cheers"

48. Cushiony

49. "If I ___ hammer . . ."

50. Auditor, for short

51. "My dog ___ fleas"

52. Calligrapher's purchase

54. Cattle call

55. "___ My Party"

57. ___ Four (Beatles)

Solution on Page 326

ACROSS

1. Former Russian space station
4. Opposite NNE
7. Resort
10. Singer Diamond
12. "Bali ___"
13. Crowd sound
14. Christmas tree decoration
16. Aide: abbr.
17. Figs.
18. Baseball card data
19. Lightens up
22. Birthday dessert
24. Pvts.' bosses
25. Can be found
28. Lay eyes on
29. Contest specifications
31. "The Eagle ___ Landed"
33. Reason to say "Gesundheit!"
35. Like skyscrapers
36. Smooth-talking
37. Harder to find
38. Every picture tells one
41. Tavern
42. Entice
43. Unrestrained
48. Aid and ___
49. Half a diam.
50. Pie-cooling spot
51. Pedal next to the brake
52. "See you later"
53. Prefix for giving or taking

DOWN

1. 6, on a phone dial
2. Suffix with cash or cloth
3. Old Japanese coin
4. "___ All That": 1999 film
5. ___ Jose
6. Sense of humor
7. Slugger Sammy
8. Bygone days
9. Music, ballet, sculpture, etc.
11. Bowling alley divisions
13. Fee schedule
15. Calendar pgs.
18. Hits the slopes
19. Letter after ar
20. Gets older
21. British gun
22. Star
23. Firefighter's tool
26. In that direction, to a whaler
27. Fifty percent off event
29. Depend (on)
30. Israeli submachine gun
32. Type of 35mm camera
34. Wading bird
35. Waterproof covers
37. Univ. dorm supervisors

228

38. Smelter residue
39. Big brass instrument
40. Underground deposits
41. Wished
43. Sphere
44. Aye's opposite
45. Canyon edge

46. Quarterback Manning
47. Letters before ems

Solution on Page 327

ACROSS

1. Hide away
6. Popular ISP
9. Pas' partners
12. Knight's weapon
13. ___-Caps (Nestlé candy)
14. AOL or MSN: abbr.
15. Get one's bearings
17. Poli-___
18. Govt. code crackers
19. Conductor's stick
21. If all ___ fails . . .
24. Tire pressure abbr.
27. Deli orders
28. Condemned's neckwear?
30. Wipe clean
32. Bearded grazer
33. Cut wood
35. Part of ITT: abbr.
38. "Halt! Who goes ___?"
40. Mall unit
42. Yearn
44. Syllable before "la la"
46. Prefix with nautical
47. Identifying tag
49. Place to enter a PIN
51. "Blessed ___ the meek . . ."
52. Equipment
58. It's between Sun. and Tue.
59. ___ Tome
60. Skip the usual wedding preparations
61. Like octogenarians
62. NNW's opposite
63. Brown-toned old photo

DOWN

1. ___-pitch softball
2. Black goo
3. "Wheel of Fortune" purchase, perhaps
4. Behind-the-___
5. Nest egg protectors?
6. Cool ___ cucumber
7. Mich. neighbor
8. "Stay" singer Lisa
9. Christmas greenery
10. High-class tie
11. Twirls
16. Strike lightly
20. Belly muscles
21. Where London is: abbr.
22. Actor Chaney
23. Home of Notre Dame
25. Underground conduit
26. Ill will
29. WNW's opposite
31. Magazine revenue source
34. Gallery display
36. Make a goof
37. Author Buscaglia

39. Bray starter

41. Tex-Mex snack

42. "Remember the ___!"

43. Christmas song

45. Org. that gets members reduced motel rates

48. Young woman

50. ___ chic

53. Faux ___

54. Edgar Allan ___

55. Summit

56. Reuters competitor

57. Caribbean, e.g.

Solution on Page 327

ACROSS

1. Totals up
5. Asner and Wynn
8. No longer worth debating
12. Second-largest Hawaiian island
13. PC linkup
14. "Jane ___"
15. Next-to-last fairy-tale word
16. Sailor's "yes"
17. "___ All Over" (Dave Clark Five hit)
18. Make a choice
20. Cenozoic or Mesozoic
22. Roebuck's partner
24. Drive up the wall
27. Desert plants
31. Emancipate
33. "___ Wanna Do" (Sheryl Crow tune)
34. El ___ (Spanish hero)
35. Choir attire
36. Accumulated
38. Having melody and harmony
39. Viet ___
40. Work, as dough
42. Bridle part
43. Stern and Newton
48. Cosby show
51. Shade maker
53. Mail-chute opening
54. Talk online
55. Sturgeon eggs
56. Prefix with hertz
57. New Haven campus
58. In a funk
59. Ladder rung

DOWN

1. Home of Iowa State
2. Pulitzer-winning humorist Barry
3. Old-fashioned showdown
4. Foal's father
5. Thrill to death
6. "The ___ of the Jackal"
7. Smiled scornfully
8. Prefix with byte
9. Olive in the comics
10. "Is it a boy ___ girl?"
11. Media mogul Turner
19. CBS police series
21. Letters after "Q"
23. All kidding ___ . . .
24. Its symbol is Fe
25. Country music's McEntire
26. Ship's backbone
27. James of "The Godfather"
28. Soprano Gluck
29. Chowder morsel
30. Frank McCourt's follow-up to "Angela's Ashes"
32. Back, once you go to

34. Midpoints
37. Go downhill fast?
38. NFL scores
41. Pointed a pistol
42. Computer unit
44. Responds on "Jeopardy!"
45. Touched down

46. ___ slaw
47. Freeze!
48. Wintry
49. ___ Na Na
50. ___ Joey
52. Mauna ___ volcano

Solution on Page 327

ACROSS

1. Beliefs
5. Swedish furniture giant
9. "It's c-c-cold!"
12. Homer Simpson's mother
13. "Ain't Misbehavin'" star Carter
14. "Ally McBeal" actress Lucy
15. ___ now (immediately)
16. Stocking ruiner
17. Running a fever
18. "Who ___ to argue?"
20. Comb-over alternative
22. Dealt leniently with
25. Speech stumbles
26. Like seawater
27. Classroom furniture
30. Mental quickness
31. Cause friction
33. Game with a jackpot
37. Look up to
40. Hockey Hall-of-Famer Bobby
41. Give some slack
42. Remained
45. Id's counterpart
46. Turkey Day day: abbr.
47. Wall Street pessimist
49. Jeans purveyor Strauss
53. Coffee dispenser
54. Bringing up the rear
55. Door-to-door cosmetics company
56. Macadamia, for one
57. Antlered animals
58. Grasped

DOWN

1. The Beatles' "___ Loser"
2. Distress call letters
3. "L–P" connection
4. African adventure
5. Not outdoors
6. Barbie's boyfriend
7. Filled with joy
8. 2000 candidate
9. Radar sign
10. Stir up
11. Golden ___
19. "A Few Good ___"
21. Ship letters
22. U-turn from NNE
23. Mop's companion
24. Voice below soprano
28. Singer Kristofferson
29. Positive
32. London's Big ___
34. Cracker Jack bonus
35. ___ clef
36. Tough time
37. Warnings
38. Man's best friend
39. Simoleons

1	2	3	4		5	6	7	8		9	10	11
12					13					14		
15					16					17		
		18	19			20		21				
22	23	24				25						
26						27			28	29		
30									31		32	
	33		34	35	36		37	38	39			
		40				41						
42	43	44					45					
46				47	48				49	50	51	52
53				54					55			
56				57					58			

42. Phaser setting

43. Drive-___ window

44. Dad's sister

48. "___ and ye shall receive"

50. First lady?

51. Remote control abbr.

52. Not Dem. or Rep.

Solution on Page 327

ACROSS

1. Advanced degree
4. Sleep phenomenon: abbr.
7. "Who ___ that masked man?"
10. Dove sounds
12. Antiquated
13. Use FedEx, say
14. Camp shelter
15. Sounds of hesitation
16. Prefix meaning trillion
17. Eight: prefix
19. Seize (from)
20. In abundance
23. A Stooge
24. Praise highly
25. Shop without buying
28. Lead-in to hap or hear
29. Old what's-___-name
30. Crow's call
32. Radio broadcast interference
35. Draw an outline of
37. Prefix with day or night
38. Hate with a passion
39. Muhammad's religion
42. Engrossed
43. Mideast canal
44. Domino dot
45. Small screen award
49. Air freshener scent
50. Average guy
51. ___ Abby
52. From Jan. 1 to now
53. Home of the NFL's Rams
54. Phone book listings: abbr.

DOWN

1. Agt.'s share
2. Clod chopper
3. Crime boss
4. MapQuest offering
5. Tickle me ___
6. AMA members
7. Cry on a roller coaster
8. Snobbish mannerisms
9. Lover's quarrel
11. Pub perch
13. Spread, as seed
18. Monitor, for short
19. Seek the affection of
20. Diamond or ruby
21. X or Y, on a graph
22. Endure
23. "___ Doubtfire"
25. Disposable-pen maker
26. "Shoo!"
27. "Hurting ___ Other" (The Carpenters)
29. Went underground
31. Itsy-bitsy
33. Astound

34. Actor Robbins

35. Spinning toy

36. Put on a scale of 1 to 10

38. Place for a squirting flower

39. '60s TV show with Bill Cosby and Robert Culp

40. Clubs or hearts

41. Give temporarily

42. Mob scene

44. Jammies

46. Stag party attendees

47. "Little Red Book" chairman

48. Twelve-mo. spans

Solution on Page 328

ACROSS

1. Middle X of X-X-X
4. Man in Eden
8. Peruvian of old
12. ___ and cry
13. Brand of blocks
14. Pastrami purveyor
15. Hoosier st.
16. Was in debt to
17. Shower with praise
18. Beer mug
20. Israel's Shimon
21. Christie of mystery
25. Smile from ear to ear
28. Miseries
29. Freud's "I"
32. Elbow's site
33. The ___ of time
34. Stocking's end
35. Bush spokesman Fleischer
36. Not a copy: abbr.
37. Buddies
38. School break
40. Get the ball rolling
44. Catchers' gloves
48. Vagrant
49. Suffix with concession
52. Dizzy Gillespie's genre
53. Gershwin's "___ Rhythm"
54. Rind
55. Anti-ICBM plan
56. Milne character
57. Hellion
58. Stovetop item

DOWN

1. Not that
2. Jemima, e.g.
3. Relinquish
4. Parallel to
5. Drops on the grass
6. Go gray, maybe
7. Stylish, in the '60s
8. Doing nothing
9. Proximate
10. Crossword hint
11. Lends a hand
19. "___ the Walrus"
20. Football throw
22. Cognizant
23. Gin's partner
24. Botanical fence
25. Sheep's plaint
26. Flub
27. "So ___!" ("Me, too!")
29. "Give ___ rest!"
30. Rank above maj.
31. For ___ a jolly good . . .
33. Put in alphabetical order
37. Letter after chi

39. Refine, as metal

40. Shape up or ___ out!

41. And miles ___ before I sleep

42. "Peek-___!"

43. IRA variety

45. Recipe meas.

46. Well-___ (prosperous)

47. Rod at a pig roast

49. NYPD alert

50. Suffix with cash, cloth, or hotel

51. Stephen of "The Crying Game"

Solution on Page 328

ACROSS

1. Lodges
5. ___ Vegas, NV
8. Goat cheese
12. Lampblack
13. Elevation: abbr.
14. Words before uproar or instant
15. ___-ran: loser
16. Perform diligently, as a trade
17. Like custard
18. Cellist Ma
19. Thumbs-up votes
21. Comedian's bit
24. Mixes
28. Eye-pleasing, as a view
31. Forbidden
32. Mideast export
33. Garden statuette
35. Wrigley Field flora
36. Distress signal
38. Scoff at
40. Beach drier
41. Gene component
42. Mama ___ of the Mamas and the Papas
45. Unappetizing food
49. Speeder's penalty
52. "Tip-Toe Thru' the Tulips With Me" instrument
54. Autumn tool
55. Not single-sex, as a school
56. What an air ball doesn't touch
57. Prepare for publication
58. Six-sided solid
59. University web address suffix
60. Peepers

DOWN

1. "___, old chap!"
2. ___ contendere: court plea
3. Intrusively curious
4. Curly or Moe
5. Full circle, on the track
6. Party to a defense pact
7. Eye annoyance
8. Cinco de Mayo party
9. Neighbor of Scot.
10. Playground game
11. Ronnie Milsap's "___ Day Now"
20. To the rear, on a ship
22. Actress Lansbury
23. Cotton ___
25. Term referring to a prev. citation
26. Bush adviser Karl
27. Tofu source
28. Missile housing
29. Crab's grabber
30. Pkg. with money due
32. Frequently, to bards
34. Kind of school

37. Inch back slowly, as a hairline

39. "Ditto!"

43. Without a doubt

44. Slide on ice

46. ___ Gaga

47. Muskogee native

48. Dogs and cats

49. Broadcast regulatory org.

50. Paper in lieu of payment

51. Omaha's home: abbr.

53. "Down Under" bird

Solution on Page 328

ACROSS

1. To a ___ (without exception)
4. No. on a bank statement
8. Sound gravelly
12. ___ roll (lucky)
13. Old TV host Jack
14. Film director Kazan
15. Singer Benatar
16. Ballet bend
17. Laura of "Jurassic Park"
18. Kind of loser
20. Prohibition agent Eliot
22. Squealer
24. Artist's rendering
28. Big bothers
32. Popular Internet company
33. ". . . boy ___ girl?"
34. Dine
36. ___ Arbor, Michigan
37. Spacek of "Coal Miner's Daughter"
40. Driver's ID
43. African desert
45. Originally named
46. Cookbook measures: abbr.
48. What a shame
51. "___ Wanna Do" (Sheryl Crow hit)
54. Swiss skiing site
56. Help!
58. Listen to
59. Actor's part
60. ___ nutshell
61. In one's right mind
62. ___ company, but three's a crowd
63. "Long ___ and far away . . ."

DOWN

1. Unruly head of hair
2. Santa ___ (hot winds)
3. Defense org. since 1949
4. Sex ___
5. Baseball iron man Ripken
6. Brother of Abel
7. Elm and oak
8. Moses parted it
9. It's poured in pints
10. "To ___, With Love"
11. Critique harshly
19. Monopoly quartet: abbr.
21. Cloud locale
23. Golf peg
25. Lighter-___-air
26. Hoodwinks
27. Make perfect
28. "Bonanza" brother
29. Sills solo
30. Accessory for Miss America
31. Actor Mineo
35. ___ Pan Alley
38. Literary spoof
39. Mos. and mos.

242

Puzzle 116

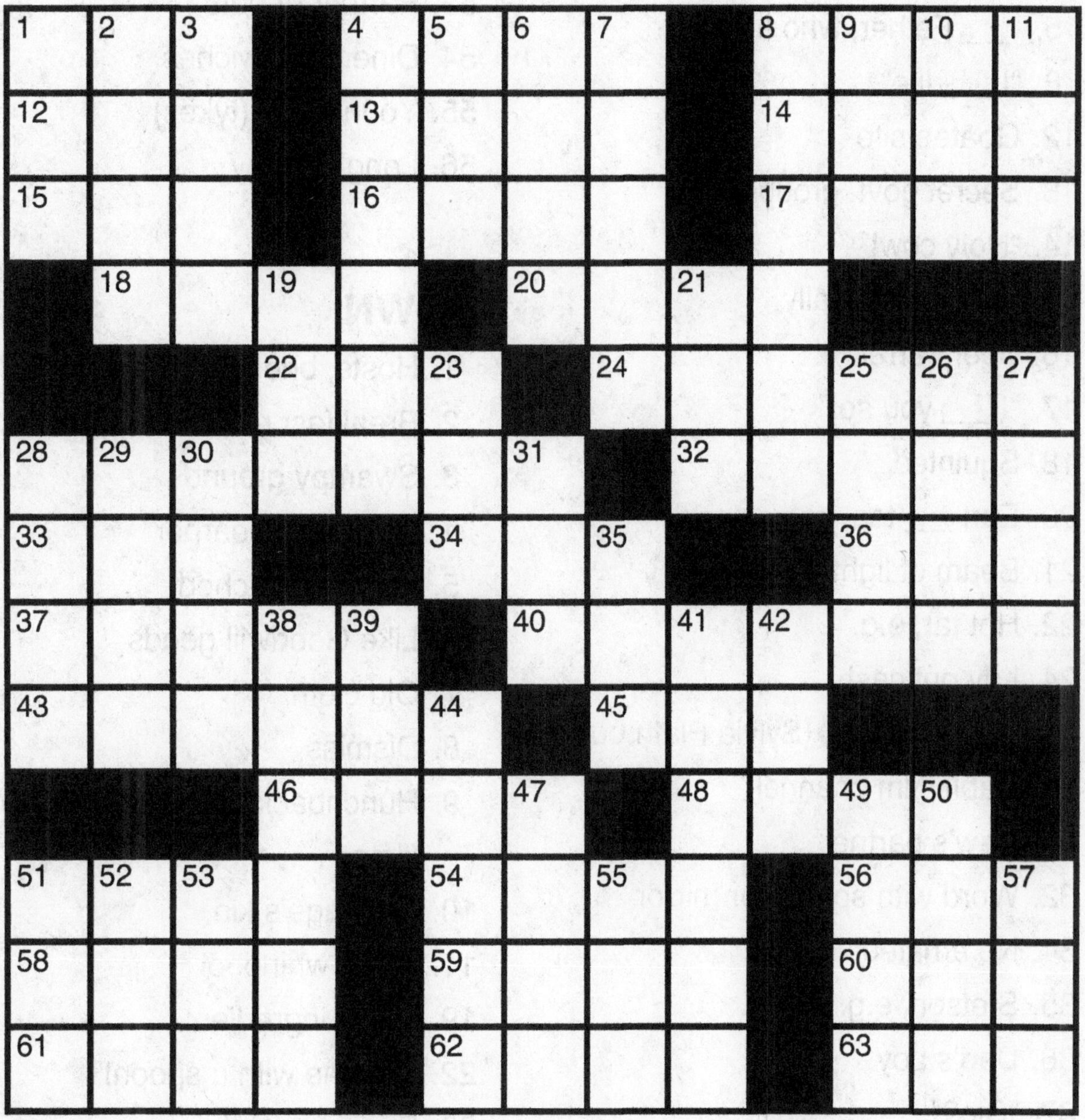

41. Puts an end to
42. Slippery one
44. Off to one side
47. Tortoiselike
49. Most populous continent
50. Something to break into
51. Relieved sounds
52. Grazing place
53. Linked-computers acronym
55. Arafat's org.
57. ___ Paulo, Brazil

Solution on Page 328

ACROSS

1. Tom's ex before Nicole
5. "___ Father, who art . . ."
8. "I ___ Ike"
12. Goatee site
13. Secret govt. group
14. "Holy cow!"
15. Arrange logically
16. Beer barrel
17. "I ___ you so!"
18. Squinted
20. Earl ___ tea
21. Beam of light
22. Hot tar, e.g.
24. Lay out cash
27. "The Bell ___" (Sylvia Plath book)
28. Cable film channel
31. Haw's partner
32. Word with spitting or mirror
34. No amateur
35. Stetson, e.g.
36. Dad's boy
37. "Dig?"
39. Bit of resistance
40. Chicago White ___
41. "To Sir With Love" singer
44. Sheets and pillowcases
47. Center of the eye
48. Cranberry-growing site
49. Vegetarians avoid it
51. Sail holder
52. Coal unit
53. Partner of pots
54. Diner sandwiches
55. Young' ___ (tykes)
56. Long journey

DOWN

1. Hosts, briefly
2. Breakfast restaurant chain
3. Swampy ground
4. On-the-job learner
5. Perfectly pitched
6. Like Goodwill goods
7. Old cloth
8. Dismiss
9. Hunchbacked assistant of horror films
10. Cabbage's kin
11. Small whirlpool
19. Salad ingredient
22. "___ me with a spoon!"
23. Eugene's state
24. Quiet, please!
25. Soup legume
26. Ambulance worker, for short
27. Feb. preceder
28. It may have 2 BR's
29. Hosp. scan
30. Barracks bunk

244

33. Dad's mate
38. Free (from)
39. Evicts
40. Omens
41. An arm or a leg
42. Russian river
43. Santa checks his twice, in song

44. Nut
45. Close by
46. Of sound mind
48. Air conditioner meas.
50. "Shame on you!"

Solution on Page 329

ACROSS

1. Aspirin target
5. Bruce Springsteen, with "The"
9. Frat party container
12. ___ upon a time . . .
13. Tennis's Arthur
14. Sailor's affirmative
15. Scent
16. Final Four org.
17. President pro ___
18. Worshiper of Brahma
20. Unsophisticated
22. Religious dissent
24. Vegas's ___ Grand
27. Approves, briefly
28. Christie's "Death on the ___"
32. Cochise or Geronimo
34. Ill will
36. Space org.
37. ___ Plaines, Illinois
38. Attila or one of his followers
39. Purple flowers
42. Incited
45. Shades
50. He floated "like a butterfly"
51. Showy flower
53. Pepsi alternative
54. Prot. or Cath.
55. Nabisco cookie
56. Voting group
57. "Live and ___ Die"
58. Kiss my grits TV diner
59. Maximum

DOWN

1. Milne bear
2. "The King ___"
3. Computer screen symbol
4. Mr. Uncool
5. Make illegal
6. Academy Awards
7. Stock unit
8. Does an usher's job
9. "Kiss Me, ___"
10. Hurricane centers
11. Rubies and such
19. This looks bad
21. Country music's Loretta
23. Barely manage, with "out"
24. "You da ___!"
25. College transcript no.
26. Barker and Bell
29. "___ liebe dich"
30. Baseball's Gehrig
31. Suffix with east or west
33. NASCAR's Yarborough
34. ___ room (play area)
35. Helper: abbr.
37. Trailblazer Boone
40. Figure of speech

41. Peter of "Casablanca"

42. Nobleman

43. Tickled-pink feeling

44. ___-edged (highest-quality)

46. Part of a nuclear arsenal, for short

47. ___ contendere

48. Ring decisions

49. Religious offshoot

52. Letters of distress

Solution on Page 329

ACROSS

1. Mom's partner
4. Kind of stick
8. RR stop
11. Death notice
13. Similar (to)
14. Favorable vote
15. Pinnacle
16. Luggage IDs
17. "All Things Considered" network: abbr.
18. Sore all over
20. Came to a close
22. Seventeen-syllable poem
25. Muddy enclosure
26. Aircraft-carrier letters
27. Check texts
30. Reverberate
34. Opener for two tins?
35. Peace Nobelist Anwar
37. Oom-___ (tuba sound)
38. Neighbor of Vietnam
40. Horsehair
41. Banking convenience, briefly
42. Docs, for short
44. Greets the day
46. Caffè with hot milk
49. Heads ___, tails . . .
51. Rankle
52. Women's golf org.
54. See-___ (transparent)
58. Sign before Virgo
59. Walked (on)
60. Weaving machine
61. Jobs for grad. students
62. Achy after a workout
63. Downing St. residents

DOWN

1. ___ good job (perform well)
2. Jackson 5 hit
3. Slow-witted
4. Way through the woods
5. Fine with me
6. Jazz job
7. First appearance, as of symptoms
8. Hourglass fill
9. Use a keyboard
10. Dweeb
12. Salad-bowl wood
19. Pool sticks
21. TV's "Science Guy" Bill
22. Toss
23. Largest continent
24. "Money ___ object!"
25. Baseball's "___ the Man"
28. Hoover and Grand Coulee
29. Snake River st.
31. Bean counters, for short
32. Love's opposite
33. Units of resistance

36. Actress Garr
39. Lt.'s subordinate
43. Animal hides
45. Worldwide: abbr.
46. Light tune
47. Region
48. Boxing wins, for short
49. Dr. Frankenstein's assistant

50. Boggs of baseball
53. Paid player
55. Short flight
56. Computer storage acronym
57. Verbal stumbles

Solution on Page 329

ACROSS

1. Money for the poor
5. ___ as a fox
8. Half: prefix
12. ___ canal (dental operation)
13. Helping hand
14. Hertz rival
15. Arrive
16. Scoreboard nos.
17. Singer Horne
18. Hwys.
20. Deuce topper
21. Together
24. Cries from creative people
27. Vice president Quayle
28. Book of maps
30. U-turn from WSW
33. Quick ___ flash
34. They're a laugh a minute
35. Hawaii's Mauna ___
36. "A Few Good ___"
37. Occupied
38. CD forerunners
39. Do one of the three Rs
40. Icy precipitation
42. Theater award
45. "Just ___ thought!"
46. Strong wind
47. Soda holder
49. Swedish auto
53. Big fibs
54. Sotheby's stock
55. Trooper prefix
56. Suffix with kitchen
57. Evening hours: abbr.
58. ___ Fifth Avenue

DOWN

1. Curve
2. London lav.
3. Oft-tattooed word
4. Back of a boat
5. Maple fluids
6. On, as a lamp
7. QB gains
8. Smelling ___
9. Eternally
10. Gold source
11. "Do as ___, not . . ."
19. Honeybunch
21. Sandler of "Big Daddy"
22. Encl. for a reply
23. ___ unrelated note . . .
24. Not silently
25. Derbies and fedoras
26. Estimate the value of
29. Singer Turner
30. Supermodel Macpherson
31. Slangy denial
32. Sunrise direction

39. Witherspoon of "Walk the Line"
41. Calls a spade a thpade
42. Make eyes at
43. Worms, for a fisherman
44. "Okay if ___ myself out?"
45. Tiny hill dwellers
47. Toy gun noisemaker

48. Limb
50. Motorist's org.
51. Noah's craft
52. English majors' degs.

Solution on Page 329

ACROSS

1. Bad ___ (German spa)
4. By the ___ of one's pants
8. Bag
12. Norma ___ (Sally Field role)
13. Synagogue scroll
14. Cousin of the bassoon
15. Engine additive letters
16. Work without ___
17. Impose, as a tax
18. Elite invitee roster
20. Valentine's Day bouquet
21. More tender
23. Clod-busting tools
25. Astronaut Shepard
26. Cooking fat
27. Speed limit abbr.
30. "Come on!"
32. Beethoven's "Moonlight ___"
34. When doubled, an African fly
35. Corporate symbol
37. "___ hardly wait!"
38. Seized vehicle
39. Windshield material
40. Number of a magazine
43. Very, very thin
45. James Brown's genre
46. Sheriff Taylor's kid
47. Hockey great Bobby
50. Masculine
51. Football officials
52. Culture-supporting org.
53. Potato
54. "Would ___ to you?"
55. Electrically charged atom

DOWN

1. Ambulance destinations, for short
2. Welcome ___
3. Divide
4. Flight of steps
5. Geologic periods
6. Franklin, known as the "Queen of Soul"
7. Make lace
8. Goes it alone
9. Beame and Burrows
10. Sheltered bay
11. Lock openers
19. Telescope part
20. Perform again
21. Pepper's partner
22. Bullfight cries
24. ". . . ___ I'm told"
26. Aerobatic maneuver
27. What Yankee Doodle called the feather
28. School grps.
29. ___ Christian Andersen
31. ___ club (singing group)

33. River where baby Moses was found

36. God's honest truth

38. Wielded authority

39. Birds in a gaggle

40. Doctrines

41. Ivory or Coast

42. "Star Trek" helmsman

44. Record player

46. ". . . ___ quit!"

48. Antique auto

49. Took off

Solution on Page 330

ACROSS

1. Photo ___ (White House events)
4. Drill insert
7. NaCl
11. Freshly painted
12. Future DA's exam
14. "Peek-___"
15. Female with a wool coat
16. Brand for Bowser
17. Greek salad cheese
18. Taste or smell
20. Track contests
22. Put a match to
23. Sun emanations
24. Hammer part
26. Consumed
27. Vigor
30. Glass container
31. Hasta la vista!
33. N.Y.C.'s Park or Madison
34. Former jrs.
35. Spy novelist Deighton
36. "Chestnuts roasting ___ open fire"
37. "Peanuts" expletive
38. British bathroom
39. Dateless
41. Film director Frank
43. Obsolescent phone feature
44. Broadway offering
46. Hi-fi component
48. Upper hand
49. Bird with a forked tail
50. Cal Tech. rival
51. Army chow
52. "___ So Fine": 1963 #1 hit
53. Literary collection

DOWN

1. Have bills
2. Church benches
3. Pittsburgh team
4. "___ From the Past"
5. ___ of Capri
6. Audible dance style
7. Vaults
8. Help in a heist
9. Real estate parcels
10. One ___ customer
13. BLT need
19. "Collages" author Anaïs
21. Looks at
23. Showers
24. Sleepwear, briefly
25. Big part of an elephant
27. Scenic view
28. A sister of Zsa Zsa
29. Animal enclosure
31. Money man Greenspan
32. Dislike with a passion
36. "Alley ___"

37. Parts to play

38. Suburban expanses

39. ___-de-camp

40. Falls behind

41. Very center

42. Dictator Idi

43. Rep.'s opponent

45. Sneaky laugh sound

47. School grp.

Solution on Page 330

ACROSS

1. Martin Sheen, to Charlie
4. Negative replies
7. Electric cord's end
11. "The X-Files" agent Scully
13. Niagara Falls' prov.
14. Submarine sandwich
15. "___ does it!"
16. "In Dreams" actor Stephen
17. Is under the weather
18. Send in payment
20. Window framework
21. Batman's sidekick
24. Mechanic's grease job
26. Stevie Wonder's "My Cherie ___"
27. "Back to the Future" actress Thompson
28. Mom's mate
31. Physics Nobelist Enrico
32. Comes to an end
34. Former "Grand Ole Opry Live" network
35. "60 Minutes" airer
38. Rice wines
39. ___ Bora (Afghan region)
40. Happening
41. Yahtzee pieces
44. Best of the best
46. Crowd noise
47. Forget-me-___

48. Please answer, on an invitation
52. Confesses, with "up"
53. Two, in Tijuana
54. Not far
55. Cracker spread
56. "___ luck?"
57. Tissue layer

DOWN

1. Banned insecticide
2. Sound of relief
3. Paternity identifier
4. Average
5. Dramatist Eugene
6. Display on a pedestal
7. Moon stage
8. "Star Wars" princess
9. Web addresses, for short
10. "Gee willikers!"
12. Open courtyard
19. Singer Caruso
21. Huck's craft
22. Sign of things to come
23. Brought into the world
25. Hound
28. ___ fun at (ridicule)
29. "___ sesame!"
30. Hushed "Hey you!"
33. Alehouse
36. Starr of the comics

37. Western pub
39. Brief and to the point
41. Plummet
42. Hawkeye State
43. Is unable to
45. Teensy
49. Calendar abbreviation

50. Kilmer who played Batman
51. Be inquisitive

Solution on Page 330

ACROSS

1. ___ dunk
5. Niagara Falls's prov.
8. Part of N.Y.C.
12. Designer Chanel
13. "Obviously!"
14. Teen affliction
15. Introductory letters?
16. "We're number ___!"
17. Smallest of a litter
18. Space streaker
20. Stoplight color
22. The British ___
24. Chop off
27. Pesto herb
31. Put in place
33. Pitcher Hershiser
34. Novelist Fleming
35. Small scissor cut
36. Put back in office
38. War's opposite
39. Tandoor-baked bread
40. Far-reaching view
42. ___ Clemente
43. Maps within maps
48. Kaput sound
51. Have supper
53. Annual theater award
54. Garfield's canine pal
55. Healthful retreat
56. In ___ land (spacy)
57. Canvas cover
58. Solar system center
59. Hides the gray

DOWN

1. Con game
2. Place for an earring
3. Bank no.
4. Pie à la ___
5. Stinks
6. "The Flying ___"
7. "___ lies a tale"
8. Ace or deuce
9. Post-op locale
10. Spike TV, formerly
11. "Are we having fun ___?"
19. Black gold
21. Inexact no.
23. Exams for future attys.
24. "The Sweater Girl" Turner
25. Suffix with hypn-
26. ___ Le Pew
27. "___ to Be Wild"
28. Length x width, for a rectangle
29. "You ain't ___ nothin' yet!"
30. Feeling poorly
32. ___ it or lose it
34. Frigidity
37. Perón of Argentina

38. Harsh review

41. Tennessee footballer

42. Stair part

44. Auctioneer's last word

45. Online auction house

46. Linoleum alternative

47. Pirates roam them

48. Flower holder

49. Pharmaceuticals' watchdog agcy.

50. Spruce relative

52. "The Simpsons" shopkeeper

Solution on Page 330

ACROSS

1. Barbed ___
5. "Survivor" network
8. Unused
11. Integrally divisible by two
12. Commencement wear
13. Rolling in dough
14. Day planner features
15. ___-Magnon
16. Sore
17. Escargot
19. Cowboy contests
21. Not straight
23. Prefix with light
24. Leave high and dry
28. It may be at the end of the tunnel
32. Maple product
33. Downs' partner
35. Big Detroit inits.
36. Sister's attire
39. Bucharest's land
42. Small bit, as of cream
44. Cleverness
45. Deep blue
48. Subject
52. Roman tyrant
53. Stanley Cup gp.
56. Constructed
57. Guitarist Atkins
58. Gosh!
59. Cast-___ stomach
60. Concealed
61. Nonprofit's URL ending
62. Boston cager, informally

DOWN

1. Dampens
2. Lendl of tennis
3. Country crooner McEntire
4. Junior naval officer
5. XXX times X
6. Saloon
7. Athletic activity
8. Delightful
9. Canyon sound
10. ___ and wherefores
13. Diameter halves
18. Boy
20. Barn bird
22. "___ Are My Sunshine"
24. Cigarette residue
25. Ewe's plaint
26. LAPD alert
27. "All Things Considered" airer
29. "Annie Get Your ___"
30. "Bali ___" ("South Pacific" song)
31. PanAm rival
34. Miss Piggy, e.g.
37. ___-proof (easy to operate)
38. "You're it!" game

40. Sch. near Harvard

41. Part of AEC

43. Drum played with the hands

45. 1/12 of a foot

46. Classic soda pop

47. ___ Scott Decision

49. Reduce, as expenses

50. Fox's "American ___"

51. Coin with Lincoln's profile

54. Billy Joel's "Tell ___ About It"

55. Relay segment

Solution on Page 331

ACROSS

1. Boast
5. Armed conflict
8. ___ reflux
12. Cotton unit
13. Roll of bills
14. Fountain drink
15. Anatomical sac
16. April 15 org.
17. Helen of ___
18. Send
20. Surmise
21. Opposite of chaos
24. Put money (on)
25. Alex Haley saga
26. Removes
30. ". . . life is ___ a dream"
31. "This weighs a ___!"
32. AOL or EarthLink, for example: abbr.
33. Child by marriage
36. Home of the NFL's Buccaneers
38. Wheel edge
39. Big tournaments
40. Banana treat
43. Eye irritation
45. Tortoise's race opponent
46. Gov. Bush's state
47. Cat's plaint
51. Self-images
52. Lithium-___ battery
53. ___ Romeo (Italian car)
54. Mardi Gras follower
55. Easter basket item
56. Little lice

DOWN

1. London TV network
2. Bit of sunshine
3. Gore and Green
4. Prepare to go
5. What V-J Day ended
6. Org. for those 50+
7. Highways: abbr.
8. Shrewd
9. Heart
10. Altar vows
11. Calendar units
19. Periods of 60 mins.
20. Toothpaste type
21. Heavenly bodies
22. Overwhelming defeat
23. Lavish affection (on)
24. Jerry's partner
26. Put on, as clothes
27. Use a stopwatch
28. Armchair athlete's channel
29. Restful resorts
31. Novelist Clancy
34. Man of the cloth

262

35. Take a load off

36. ___ with (tease)

37. Tarzan, for one

40. Author Silverstein

41. Senate errand runner

42. Scientologist ___ Hubbard

43. Plod through the mud

44. Sharp flavor

46. "Fee, ___, fo, fum"

48. Peyton Manning's younger brother

49. Many a time

50. "___ it something I said?"

Solution on Page 331

ACROSS

1. ___ Butterworth's
4. Ump.'s call
8. "___ Lama Ding Dong"
12. Road service org.
13. Author Leon
14. Annual checkup
15. Zippo
16. Desserts with crusts
17. Baptism or bar mitzvah
18. Main course
20. Tickles the fancy
22. WWW address
23. Longing for Japanese money?
24. Molt
27. Alternative to unleaded: abbr.
28. Banned spray
31. Jukebox choice
32. Reel's partner
33. Author Angelou
34. Chicken drumstick
35. Cornhusker St.
36. "Wait ___!"
37. Theater admonition
38. Maid's cloth
40. Longhorns, e.g.
43. Singer Newton-John
47. Dull hurt
48. "Alas!"
50. "___ Be Home for Christmas"
51. Gather, as grain
52. Part of a wedding cake
53. Calendar abbr.
54. Buyer beware phrase
55. Good name for a Dalmatian
56. From point ___ point B

DOWN

1. Lion's hair
2. Drought relief
3. Potato chip seasoning
4. "Great!"
5. Disney's "Little Mermaid"
6. Old expression of disgust
7. Made an attempt
8. Second airing
9. Graph's x or y
10. Chess finale
11. Home of Iowa State University
19. Boorish
21. Ryan of "Sleepless in Seattle"
24. Letters on a "Cardinals" cap
25. Shade
26. High school subj.
27. Stick up
28. "___ Boot" (1981 war film)
29. Recolor
30. Tic-toe connector
32. Warms up again
33. Biblical wise men

264

35. Stanley Cup org.

37. Staircase units

38. Juliet's beloved

39. Open-eyed

40. Irene of "Fame"

41. Perfect serves

42. Bangkok native

44. MasterCard alternative

45. "Okay if ___ myself out?"

46. Brand for Fido

49. "With it"

Solution on Page 331

ACROSS

1. Sawyer or Seaver
4. Scrooge's cry
7. Kind of PC monitor
10. Prefix with morphosis
11. Freud subject
12. Words of surprise
14. Hammer's target
15. Rep.'s foe
16. "___ Man" (Estevez film)
17. Academy Award
19. Input data again
21. It's like "-like"
23. Letters before a pseudonym
24. Pupil of Plato
28. Frequently, to a bard
31. ___ one's time (wait)
32. ___ can play that game
33. Auto with a four-ring logo
34. "60 Minutes" network
35. Rob Reiner's mock rock band
37. "Blame It on ___" (Caine film)
38. Prefix with gram or center
39. Confronts boldly
43. Mississippi River transport
47. Stop!
48. &
50. Chimney buildup
51. They're kissable
52. Road cover
53. Household power: abbr.
54. Cool dude, in jazz
55. Photo ___: publicity events
56. Camera initials

DOWN

1. Celestial Seasonings selections
2. Suffix with psych-
3. The blahs
4. Four-poster, e.g.
5. Ending for "teen"
6. 1990 Macaulay Culkin film
7. "___ Doone" (1869 novel)
8. Atkins of country music
9. Narc.'s seizure
10. Pre-"P" three
13. Opposite of vert.
18. "Q–U" link
20. Scratch (out)
22. Something dropped
24. Alphabet openers
25. Chest protector
26. Proofs of age, for short
27. Prefix with night or light
28. ___ of bounds
29. Rx watchdog org.
30. Redcap's reward
33. Assumed names
35. Female sib
36. Police alert, for short

37. Celebrity skewering

39. Hole punching tool

40. Trendy

41. Nightclub in a Manilow tune

42. Ginger cookie

44. Rock's partner

45. Ending for "theater" or "church"

46. And others: abbr.

49. Welby and Kildare: abbr.

Solution on Page 331

ACROSS

1. Moms
4. Jar part
7. Powerful punch
11. "___ Got the World on a String"
12. Soul singer Redding
14. Peel
15. Bon ___: witticism
16. Basketball's Archibald
17. Wheel turner
18. Tooth layer
20. ___ of the line
22. Not sweet, as wine
23. ___ Peanut Butter Cups
27. Copper-zinc alloy
30. Make clothes
31. Olive ___
32. "Ticket to ___"
33. Degree held by many univ. professors
34. Singer Irene
35. "Here ___ again!"
36. "Now I ___ me down to sleep . . ."
37. "The Taming of the ___"
38. School papers
40. Cutie ___
41. Ping-Pong table divider
42. Printed mistakes
46. Linkletter and Garfunkel
49. Suffix with major
51. No thanks
52. Stalactite site
53. Onion covering
54. Words before "You may kiss the bride"
55. Blue-green hue
56. Tiebreaking periods, briefly
57. Not yea

DOWN

1. Marcel Marceau, e.g.
2. Bell-ringing cosmetics company
3. ___ precedent
4. Recluses
5. Milan's land
6. Morse code word
7. Black card
8. Calif. airport
9. Web address: abbr.
10. "___ whiz!"
13. Get really steamed
19. Store goods: abbr.
21. First word in four state names
24. Fly like an eagle
25. Brontë's "Jane ___"
26. Cole ___
27. Cheese on crackers
28. Big trucks
29. Bustles
30. Like a shrinking violet

33. Puts in the scrapbook

34. Sonny's partner

36. Strong alkaline

37. Air-raid warnings

39. Wilderness photographer Adams

40. ___ four (teacake)

43. Has ___ with (knows)

44. Dramatic entrance announcement

45. Cry to a matey

46. Do something

47. "Norma ___" (Field film)

48. New Deal agcy.

50. Ring decision, briefly

Solution on Page 332

ACROSS

1. Mary had a little one
5. Overhead trains
8. Bamboozle
12. R.E.M.'s "The ___ Love"
13. Counterpart of long.
14. Sale tag caution
15. Animal with a beard
16. Lumberjack's tool
17. Johnny of "Pirates of the Caribbean"
18. Goes in
20. Conductor Previn
22. Egypt's King ___
23. F major or E minor
24. Disneyland's locale
28. Foil maker
32. Nat King ___
33. New Deal agcy.
35. On the ___ (not speaking)
36. Cree or Crow
38. Blue feeling
40. Merchandise ID
42. Actress Ryan
43. ___ as a rock
45. Join the military
49. Delinquent GI
50. Aunt or uncle: abbr.
52. Suffix with kitchen or luncheon
53. Jimi Hendrix hit "Purple ___"
54. Tic-tac-toe nonwinner
55. Old Pontiacs
56. Encourage in crime
57. Got together
58. Second-year student, for short

DOWN

1. Seating section
2. Author unknown, for short
3. Potatoes' partner
4. Prepare for unpleasantness
5. Stretchy, as a waistband
6. CA airport
7. T-bone, e.g.
8. Spiderlike bug
9. ___-friendly (easy to operate)
10. Sherlock Holmes item
11. Sixth sense letters
19. ___ the day
21. Cultural funding grp.
24. Perform on stage
25. ". . . ___ a lender be"
26. "Float like a butterfly, sting like a bee" boxer
27. Banquet hosts: abbr.
29. Pool stick
30. NFL tiebreakers
31. Long-eared beast of burden
34. King Arthur's home
37. Prefix with center

Puzzle 130

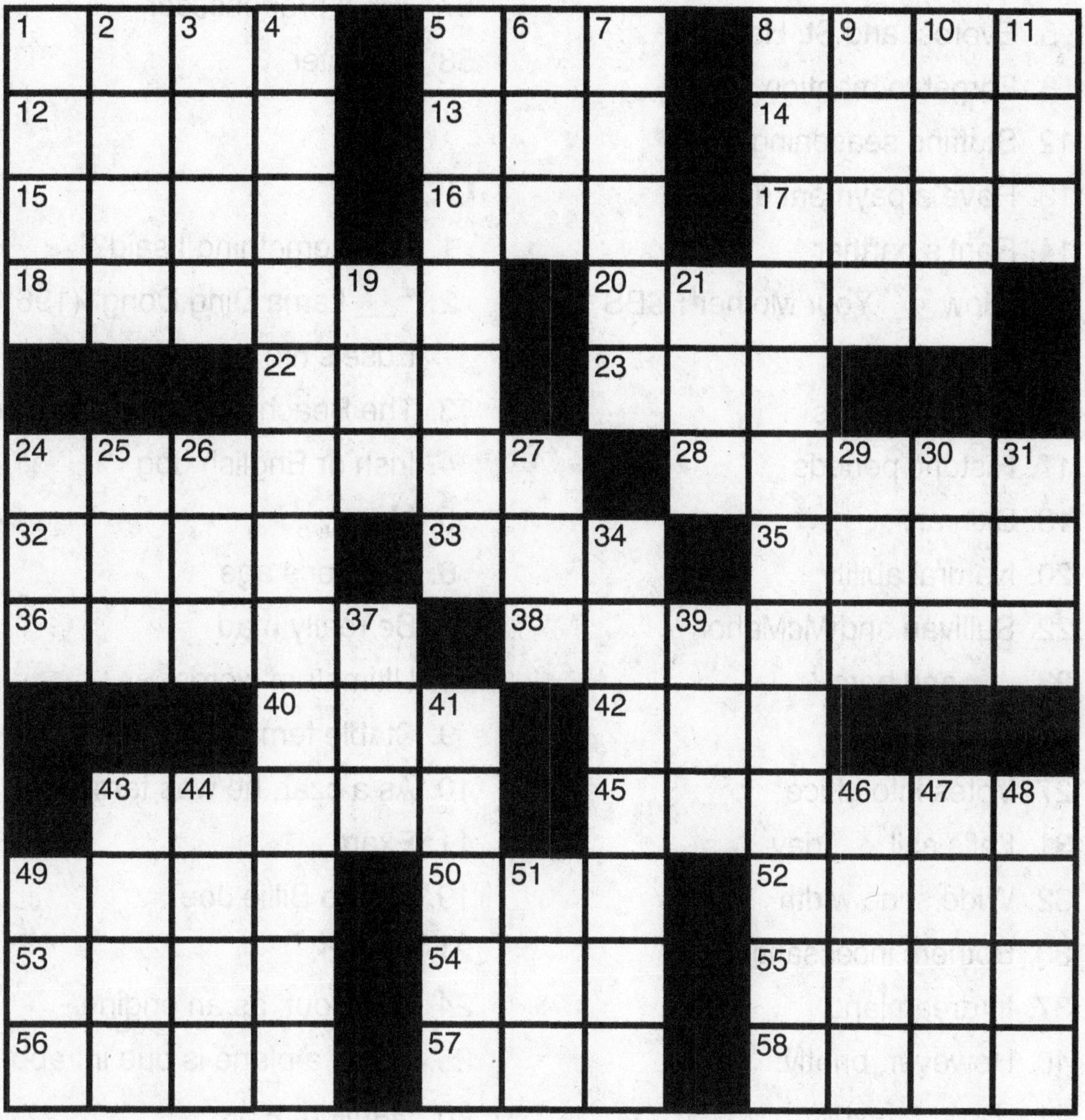

39. Group of Cub Scouts
41. PC storage medium
43. Clean the deck
44. Leak slowly
46. "What's ___ you?"
47. "That's enough!"
48. Former "Entertainment Tonight" host
49. "Now I understand!"
51. Computer file name extension

Solution on Page 332

ACROSS

1. Colored eye part
5. Everest and St. Helens
8. Forget to mention
12. Stuffing seasoning
13. Have a payment due
14. Rant's partner
15. "How ___ Your Mother": CBS sitcom
16. Precious eggs
17. Historic periods
18. Skin art
20. Natural ability
22. Sullivan and McMahon
23. ___ and hers
24. Edict
27. Votes into office
31. Let's call ___ day
32. Wide shoe width
33. Bothers incessantly
37. In dreamland
40. However, briefly
41. "Do ___ favor"
42. Emphasize
45. Angel hair and penne
49. Bank transaction
50. That's all ___ wrote
52. ___ out: betray
53. "I'm ___ your tricks!"
54. A barber has to work around it
55. Eight: prefix
56. Honey makers
57. JFK's predecessor
58. Imposter

DOWN

1. "___ something I said?"
2. "___ Lama Ding Dong" (1961 Edsels hit)
3. The Beach Boys' "___ Around"
4. Irish or English dog
5. Moody
6. Toddler's age
7. Be really mad
8. Ultimatum words
9. Stable female
10. As a czar, he was terrible
11. Exam
19. "___ to Billie Joe"
21. Be sick
24. Conk out, as an engine
25. When a plane is due in: abbr.
26. Garfield, e.g.
28. Bee follower
29. ___ time (golf course slot)
30. Fall mo.
34. Dictation takers
35. Sounds of satisfaction
36. Like some salads
37. Electric current unit

272

38. Dead ___ Scrolls

39. Rodeo ropes

42. Messy dresser

43. Dial sound

44. Distance divided by time

46. Part of MIT: abbr.

47. ___ Vista (Internet search engine)

48. Close angrily

51. "This ___ better be good!"

Solution on Page 332

ACROSS

1. Acquire
4. "Wheel of Fortune" purchase
7. Jack Horner's find
11. Paul Bunyan's tool
12. ___-pattern baldness
14. In need of a map
15. Geometric curve
17. Thumbs-up votes
18. "8 Mile" rapper
19. Boy king of Egypt
21. Half of hex-
22. Oscar winner Jeremy ___
25. Excavates
28. Cable news source
29. Wire service inits.
31. With competence
32. Harbor vessel
33. Similar
34. Gambling cube
35. Bark sharply
36. Microscope part
37. Interior design
39. Super Bowl org.
41. Daiquiri base
42. Starting point
46. Ferris wheel or bumper cars
49. Estrange
51. Barely gets by, with "out"
52. Players in a play
53. Column crosser
54. Units of length
55. Thriller director Craven
56. B&O and Union Pacific

DOWN

1. Stare
2. Crammer's concern
3. Bond girl Hatcher
4. Yellowish-brown
5. Mama Judd
6. Ailing
7. Follower of Socrates
8. "The Thin Man" actress
9. Put to good ___
10. McKinley, Hood, et al.: abbr.
13. Restaurant activity
16. Unable to sit still
20. Large coffee maker
23. Cook in the microwave
24. ___ the bottle
25. Father
26. As before, in footnotes
27. Elation
28. Java holder
30. Shoo-___ (sure things)
32. Airport surface
33. It's ___ a day's work
35. Last word of the golden rule
38. Top of a wave

274

39. "Let's make some ___!"
40. Guitar bars
43. Teri of "Close Encounters of the Third Kind"
44. "Believe ___ not!"
45. Front-page stuff
46. Gridiron official, for short

47. ___ & Tina Turner Revue
48. Actor Billy ___ Williams
50. Perry Mason's profession

Solution on Page 332

ACROSS

1. Supplies with weapons
5. Outward flow
8. Let fall
12. Hen pen
13. Kauai keepsake
14. Data, for short
15. Love ___ leave it
16. It's all the rage
17. Bank fixture
18. He loved Lucy
19. "Semper Fi" org.
21. Neighbor of Aus.
24. Major artery
28. Lend a hand to
31. Sign gases
34. Self-proclaimed psychic Geller
35. Owl's question?
36. Diamond weight
37. Cargo weight
38. "Man of a Thousand Faces" Chaney
39. Hit from Grandpa's day
40. Producer's dream
41. Thrown weapon
43. Train lines: abbr.
45. "Smoke ___ in Your Eyes"
48. VCR insert
52. Sunrise
55. Since Jan. 1
57. Comedian King
58. "The Andy Griffith Show" boy
59. Pea's home
60. Saturn feature
61. Phoenix hoopsters
62. Be behind in payments
63. Fortuneteller

DOWN

1. Etching liquid
2. Learning method
3. Dairy farm sounds
4. Parsley portion
5. North Pole toy maker
6. Steady guy
7. Auction actions
8. Place to do the hustle
9. Genetic material
10. Popular insect repellent
11. "Once upon a midnight dreary" writer
20. Top chess player
22. "One more time!"
23. Genuine
25. Baseball's Bambino
26. "Star Trek": TNG counselor
27. "___ That a Shame"
28. Piercing tools
29. Breakfast chain
30. Finished

276

32. Chicago airport code
33. Neet rival
42. Actress Moorehead
44. Constellation components
46. Printing goof
47. Pack away
49. "That's ___!" ("Not true!")

50. Window section
51. MIT grad
52. Uno + uno
53. Storekeeper on "The Simpsons"
54. Get a blue ribbon
56. HST's successor

Solution on Page 333

ACROSS

1. Yes, in Yokohama
4. Rice Krispies sound
8. Homecoming attendee, for short
12. Ash holder
13. "See you," in Sorrento
14. Wave type
15. Queue after A
16. "Be ___!" ("Help me out!")
17. Bird's home
18. Wolf's sound
20. Optometrist's interest
22. Moss or Gary
25. Great Lakes Indians
29. Merle Haggard's "___ From Muskogee"
32. "___ Rock" (Simon & Garfunkel hit)
34. "I Pity the Fool" star
35. It's part of growing up
38. Hole-punching tool
39. "All You ___ Is Love"
40. Subj. for Milton Friedman
41. Cousin of lavender
43. Country's McEntire
45. Four-poster, e.g.
47. "___ Well That Ends Well"
50. Clinton's veep
53. Send out, as rays
56. Mo. with no holidays
58. Castle fortification
59. All's opposite
60. ___-Blo fuses
61. Hanks and Cruise
62. Oodles
63. Quonset ___

DOWN

1. Wheel's center
2. Part of a foot
3. ___-European languages
4. Milan's La ___
5. ___ in the bud
6. Battery size
7. Barbershop emblem
8. Ed of "Lou Grant"
9. Fib
10. Young'___ (kids)
11. Happened upon
19. Roller coaster cry
21. Affirmative votes
23. Prevalent
24. Become narrower
26. Apple computer
27. Hence
28. British weapon of WWII
29. Not written
30. Green fruit
31. "___ be a cold day in . . ."
33. ___-to-order (custom)

278

36. "___ upon a time . . ."

37. Close tightly

42. Aids and ___

44. "Psycho" motel name

46. Fender-bender result

48. Place for mascara

49. "Star Trek" navigator

50. London hrs.

51. Winning tic-tac-toe row

52. Aries animal

54. ___ goo gai pan

55. Bed-and-breakfast

57. Obtained

Solution on Page 333

ACROSS

1. The Beatles' "Let ___"
5. RR depot
8. Norm: abbr.
11. Furrowed part of the head
12. Mai ___ (tropical drink)
13. Swing in the breeze
14. Maxi's opposite
15. Series of scenes
16. Reebok rival
17. Eventually
20. Come together
21. Rowboat blade
22. NFL gains
25. Kipling novel
27. River mouth formation
31. Pink wine
33. Tetley product
35. Staircase part
36. Bloodhound's clue
38. "For shame!"
40. Banned insecticide, for short
41. Stove option
43. Caspian or Caribbean
45. Saver of nine
52. It's clicked on a computer
53. Univ. dorm overseers
54. Cheers for the matador
55. Created
56. Insect on a hill
57. Walk with a hitch
58. ___ Cone (summer treat)
59. Rx prescribers
60. Exodus author Uris

DOWN

1. Certain computers
2. Threesome
3. Sonny of Sonny and Cher
4. "Dallas" family name
5. Like a clear night sky
6. Crunchy Mexican treat
7. Explosive liquid, for short
8. Houlihan portrayer
9. Seize
10. Hair colorer
13. Entraps
18. Mouse hater's cry
19. Young chap
22. Periods of 52 wks.
23. Bandleader Severinsen
24. 180 degrees from NNW
26. Encountered
28. Old Ford model
29. CNN founder Turner
30. Prone
32. Wankel or diesel
34. Helps out
37. "I tawt I taw a puddy ___"
39. Barbie's guy

42. "Git!"

44. Bikini Island, e.g.

45. Points (at)

46. Read bar codes

47. Heading on a list of chores

48. Something to shake with

49. Nastase of tennis

50. Office note

51. Sports cable network

Solution on Page 333

ACROSS

1. Beach bum's shade
4. Mafia boss
8. Bug-eyed
12. Palette selection
13. "Wait just ___!"
14. Shoe bottom
15. $$$ dispenser
16. Coin factory
17. Barbershop touch-up
18. Nary a soul
20. 2004 Olympics site
22. Part of TGIF: abbr.
24. Moon vehicle
25. Mascara site
29. Two under par
33. Poker prize
34. Kitten's plaint
36. Small amount
37. Ancient Peruvians
40. Justifications
43. Industrial container
45. Genetic stuff
46. Assert without proof
49. Lip application
53. Wedding cake layer
54. "No time to wallow in the ___"
    (Doors lyric)
57. Nova subj.
58. "___ a man with seven wives"
59. Serve coffee
60. "The Cat in the ___"
61. Golfers' goals
62. Inning enders
63. Sit-up targets

DOWN

1. Comparison word
2. Car
3. Disney clownfish
4. Tripod topper
5. Faulkner's "___ Lay Dying"
6. Mont Blanc, e.g.
7. Based on eight
8. Respiratory problem
9. Clinton's no. 2
10. Actress Lena
11. Precious stones
19. Gridiron grp.
21. ___ time (course slot)
23. Any doctrine
25. Prefix for center
26. Over there, poetically
27. And so on: abbr.
28. "How Stella Got ___ Groove Back"
30. Powerful Pontiac
31. PC data-sharing system
32. Mag. workers
35. Tie the knot
38. Turns away

Puzzle 136

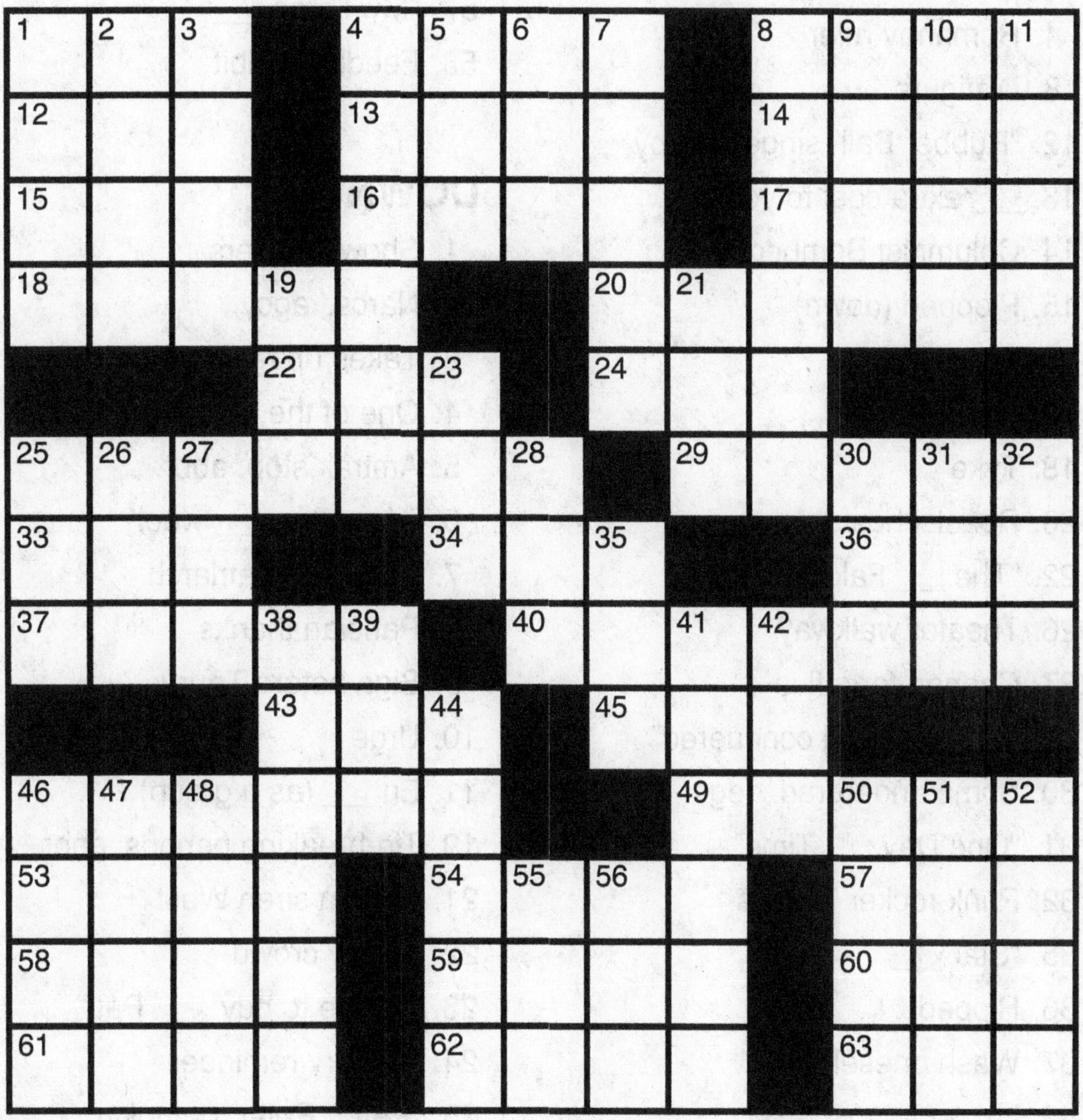

39. Sink in the middle
41. Makes mad
42. Erie Canal mule
44. Musical pace
46. "Let me give you ___"
47. Peru's largest city
48. Lusty look
50. Safety org.
51. Picket-line crosser
52. Uses a stool
55. Promissory initials
56. Truck track

Solution on Page 333

ACROSS

1. NFL six-pointers
4. Romanov ruler
8. Disfigure
12. "Rubber Ball" singer Bobby
13. ___ extra cost to you
14. Columnist Bombeck
15. Plopped (down)
16. Verbalizes
17. Tears
18. Tyke
20. Roasts' hosts
22. "The ___ Falcon"
26. Theater walkway
27. Change for a five
28. "I ___, I saw, I conquered"
30. Some undergrad. degs.
31. "One Day ___ Time"
32. Punk rocker Vicious
35. "Star ___"
36. Ripped
37. Wash oneself
41. Let go
43. UFO crew
45. Writer Fleming
46. Rich soil
47. Bedazzles
50. Lah-di-___
53. Blood fluids
54. Geezer
55. Glide over snow
56. Wise ___ owl
57. "My Three ___"
58. Feedbag tidbit

DOWN

1. Show showers
2. Narcs.' agcy.
3. Takes up residence (in)
4. One of the senses
5. Amtrak stop: abbr.
6. "Have you ___ wool?"
7. Kennedy matriarch
8. Parisian thanks
9. Sign before Taurus
10. Urge
11. En ___ (as a group)
19. Tie-breaking periods: abbr.
21. Screen siren West
22. Unruly crowd
23. "I'd like to buy ___, Pat!"
24. Surgery reminder
25. "Peter, Peter, pumpkin ___ . . ."
29. "___ my day!"
32. Blankety-blank type
33. Tax org.
34. Fiddle-de-___
35. Perfect Olympics score
36. Mad Hatter's drink
37. Model airplane wood

284

38. Medicinal plants

39. Pageant crown

40. Macho dude

42. Shopping aids

44. Pouches

48. Wine and dine

49. Long period of time

51. Wanted poster abbr.

52. Batter's goal

Solution on Page 334

ACROSS

1. Cut, as nails
5. ___ and ye shall receive
8. Dinner from a bucket
12. Cat-o'- ___ -tails
13. Sheep's bleat
14. Game with mallets
15. Microwave
16. Coal container
17. Omelet ingredients
18. Winter coat material
20. Jacket
21. London's Royal ___ Hall
24. "Now, where ___ I?"
26. "Two Women" star Sophia
27. Popular tattoo
28. Capote, on Broadway
31. Airport overseer: abbr.
32. ___ acid (protein component)
34. ___ of 1812
35. "The Joy Luck Club" writer Tan
36. April 15 payment
37. Have the throne
39. Country singer Ritter
40. Prickly plant
41. Ready for picking
44. Telephone inventor
45. Aches and pains
46. Perfect gymnastics score
47. "Should ___ acquaintance . . ."
51. Get together
52. Krazy ___
53. Polo shirt brand
54. "Don't go!"
55. Takes too much, briefly
56. Barbecue offerings

DOWN

1. "Larry King Live" channel
2. Lucy of "Charlie's Angels," 2000
3. Bic filler
4. Miniature
5. Monastery head
6. Go yachting
7. Alternative to KS
8. Eyeglasses, for short
9. NBC's peacock, e.g.
10. Korbut of the 1972 Olympics
11. Fence stake
19. Richly decorated
21. ___ Romeo
22. Gardener's soil
23. Jackass's sound
24. Took the gold
25. Without principles
27. Blend
28. Nincompoop
29. Brand of spaghetti sauce
30. Coffee containers
33. To the ___ (fully)

38. Oblong cream puff

39. Short-tempered

40. Pennies

41. Edges

42. "Sorry if ___ you down"

43. "Not guilty," e.g.

44. Rosary component

46. Bout stopper, for short

48. Israeli gun

49. Soft toss

50. Driller's deg.

Solution on Page 334

ACROSS

1. Roadies carry them
5. "I ___ Rock" (Simon & Garfunkel hit)
8. Sewing connection
12. Actor Brad
13. Swift boat vets' war
14. Big stack
15. "___ does it"
16. Yea's opposite
17. "I'm working ___"
18. Claim on property
20. Fence supports
21. ___ ego
24. Roald who wrote "James and the Giant Peach"
26. Little hoppers
27. "Invasion of the Body Snatchers" container
28. ___-mo (instant replay feature)
31. Hockey's Bobby
32. Good friend
33. Moon jumper of rhyme
34. ___ culpa
35. Tibetan ox
36. ___ tectonics
38. Broadway "Auntie"
39. Leases
40. Homeless animal
43. "And ___ There Were None"
45. Oaf

46. Words before glance or loss
47. Fly alone
51. Going ___ (fighting)
52. Winter ailment
53. Observer
54. Femur or fibula
55. Rolodex no.
56. Glided

DOWN

1. Mimic
2. Soccer star Hamm
3. Score components: abbr.
4. Fashioned
5. Actress Bancroft
6. Rustic film couple
7. Singer Grant
8. Thread holder
9. German one
10. Came down to Earth
11. New York nine
19. Form 1040 org.
20. Prof.'s degree
21. Molecule part
22. Traditional knowledge
23. The O'Hara homestead
25. "You've got mail" co.
28. CAT ___
29. Mississippi's Trent
30. Is in arrears

32. Actress Dawber
35. "Whoopee!"
36. Before: prefix
37. Telescope parts
38. Dull photo finish
40. Thick slice
41. "The Wizard of Oz" dog

42. Archaeological site
44. Tow
46. Toward the stern
48. Popeye's Olive ___
49. Floral necklace
50. California's Fort ___

Solution on Page 334

ACROSS

1. Contentedly confident
5. Wise bird
8. Undercover agent
11. Cupid's projectile
13. Letterman's "Stupid ___ Tricks"
14. On the ___: fleeing
15. Oscar who wrote "The Picture of Dorian Gray"
16. Little bit
17. Ltd., in the States
18. Work hard
20. Pasture sound
21. "___: Miami" (David Caruso series)
24. %: abbr.
25. Moon-roving vehicle
26. A large quantity
29. "Big Love" airer
31. French ___ soup
32. Synagogue leader
36. New Deal dam-building org.
38. Selects from the menu
39. "I tawt I taw a puddy ___!"
41. Bench with a back
43. Opening
44. Not happy
45. Pub measure
47. Unit of resistance
48. Rule, for short
49. Notre Dame's Fighting ___

54. "The Fall of the House of Usher" writer
55. Oom-___ band
56. Engine
57. Barnyard cackler
58. Chain-wearing "A-Team" actor
59. Unruly groups

DOWN

1. Glimpsed
2. X-ray alternative
3. Dot-com's address
4. Deity
5. Eye-related
6. Riches
7. Inc., in Britain
8. Icky residue
9. Bygone airline
10. 1978 hit with the lyric "You can get yourself clean, you can have a good meal"
12. Dampen
19. Photo ___ (PR events)
21. Dove sound
22. Bush 43, to Bush 41
23. Dictator Amin
25. Put bullets in
27. Senator Trent
28. Letter holder: abbr.
30. Reaction to the cold
33. Ask for alms

34. Playtex item

35. AOL, e.g.: abbr.

37. Come into view

38. Possess

39. Nevada resort

40. Madison Avenue types

42. Two cubed

44. Former frosh

46. Director Burton

48. 33 or 45, e.g.

50. CD-___

51. Judge Lance ___

52. Blubber

53. "48 ___" (Nick Nolte film)

Solution on Page 334

ACROSS

1. "___ you ready?"
4. Breaks bread
8. Part of E.U.: abbr.
11. Rat (on)
13. "___ Girl" (TV show)
14. Letters after "L"
15. Akron's home
16. Head covering
17. Vet.'s patient
18. Prickly plant
20. Cowboy's rope
22. Kind of salad
23. Analyze, as a sentence
24. Hosp. areas
25. Hide-and-___
28. Adolescent
29. "The Canterbury ___"
31. Narrow street
35. Folk tales and such
36. Author Fleming or McEwan
39. Limber
41. Juice source
43. "Gentlemen ___ Blondes"
45. Gives some lip
46. Instant, for short
47. Get higher
49. Repressed, with "up"
50. Wide shoe spec
51. Put ___ appearance

52. "The Sweetest Taboo" singer
53. Dental deg.
54. Rim
55. Alfred E. Neuman's magazine

DOWN

1. Immediately
2. Try again, as a court case
3. Upper crusts
4. Celestial
5. Opposite of "Huh?"
6. Party game pin-on
7. Subway handhold
8. "The ___ Strikes Back"
9. Nervousness
10. Spoiled
12. Oodles
19. ___, but not least . . .
21. Lab maze runner
26. "Xanadu" rock grp.
27. Lamp fuel
30. Will be, in a Doris Day song
31. Was not renewed
32. Shook hands (on)
33. Sisters' daughters
34. Santa's helper
36. Pants measurement
37. Meeting plan
38. Fitted one within another
40. Spine-chilling

42. Vipers

44. Lemon peel

48. Lose firmness

Solution on Page 335

ACROSS

1. Computer input
5. Lobbying grp.
8. Swedish soprano Jenny
12. Fired
13. ___ thumbs: clumsy
14. Wild hog
15. Downhill racer
16. Restore confidence to
18. Female fowl
19. Deputized group
20. Biol. or anat.
21. Adam's second son
23. Lucky rabbit's foot, e.g.
25. Make null and void
27. Horse sense
31. Has debts
32. Song for one
33. Mother ___
36. In one piece
38. Lawn base
39. Owner's proof
40. Trojans' sch.
43. Thesaurus compiler
45. U.K. military fliers
48. Flowering vine
50. Cry from a crib
51. Not mom's
52. Business card no.
53. Bakery worker
54. King Kong's kin
55. Sophs., two years later
56. Hereditary carrier

DOWN

1. Sprint
2. Wheel shaft
3. Adolescent
4. Tally (up)
5. Conditional release from prison
6. Saloon orders
7. Necklace fasteners
8. Weight abbr.
9. Cash substitutes
10. Drug cop
11. Eins, zwei, ___
17. Line of stitches
19. Caress
22. First, second, third, and home
24. ___ not, want not
25. "Believe It or ___!"
26. Lamb's mother
28. Grand Prix, e.g.
29. Compassionate letters
30. Barfly
34. Alphabetize, e.g.
35. Takes into one's family
36. Standards of perfection
37. Badminton court divider
40. Fed. food inspectors

41. Trade

42. Hand over

44. Will of "The Walton's"

46. End of a prayer

47. Price of a ride

49. Superman's symbol

50. Russian plane

Solution on Page 335

ACROSS

1. Rd. or hwy.
4. Leary's drug
7. ___-relief sculpture
10. Fourth-down option
12. Letters after els
13. Composer Johann Sebastian
14. Like feudal times
16. Guthrie who sang "Alice's Restaurant"
17. Postal delivery
18. Follow as a consequence
19. Tough question
22. Princess who battles the Death Star
24. Opposed to
25. Mark Twain, for Samuel Clemens
29. Radio host Don
30. Eggy drink
31. Have ___ with (know well)
32. Beef, e.g.
34. Walkman maker
35. Gymnast Korbut
36. Sleep problem
37. Reads, as a bar code
40. Bridge-crossing fee
42. ___ de foie gras
43. Mexican food staple
47. Like many independent films
48. Half a laugh
49. Animator's creation
50. Secret agent
51. Recent immigrant's class: abbr.
52. Hither's partner

DOWN

1. Meas. of engine speed
2. Mon. follower
3. Conclusion
4. ___ Strauss & Co.
5. Something of trivial importance
6. High-speed Internet letters
7. Happy hour stops
8. Rights advocacy org.
9. Loafer or moccasin
11. Manager's catchphrase
13. Dairy Queen offering
15. Lobe site
18. Ich bin ___ Berliner: JFK
19. Twosome
20. "Drinks are ___!"
21. Variety of poker
23. Brain-scan letters
26. Shortly
27. Selfish one's exclamation
28. "Orinoco Flow" singer
30. Over-the-hill horse
33. Raised railways
36. Flight height: abbr.
37. Healthful retreats

38. Peevish complaint

39. Lawyer: abbr.

41. Hershiser on the mound

43. Most common English word

44. Myrna of "The Thin Man"

45. WC

46. Late columnist Landers

Solution on Page 335

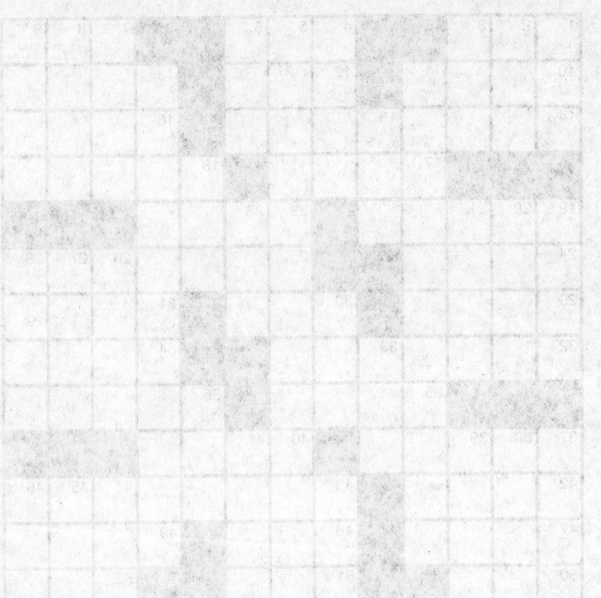

Answers

Puzzle 1

```
S H U T . E B B S . U G H
O O Z E . G O O N . C R Y
T W I N . G O N E . L I P
. . . O J S . A G A P E .
A D O R E . L I K E . . .
M A X . D I O N . R O B S
F L E W . C U T . M A L E
M Y N A . K I L N . R U N
. . . G A Y E . B E S E T
T W E E N . . L A X . . .
R I N . I N K Y . A C D C
O T C . M I L E . M A Y O
D S L . E L M S . S P E W
```

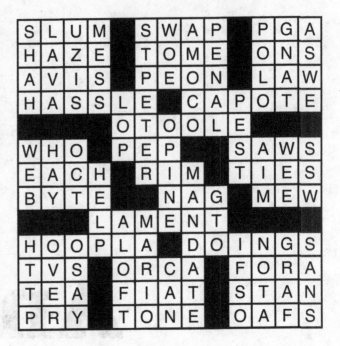

Puzzle 2

```
S L U M . S W A P . P G A
H A Z E . T O M E . O N S
A V I S . P E O N . L A W
H A S S L E . C A P O T E
. . . O T O O L E . . . .
W H O . P E P . S A W S .
E A C H . R I M . T I E S
B Y T E . N A G . M E W .
. . L A M E N T . . . . .
H O O P L A . D O I N G S
T V S . O R C A . F O R A
T E A . F I A T . S T A N
P R Y . T O N E . O A F S
```

Puzzle 3

```
T W I . S C H . . S O U P
R E D . P E A S . H I R E
U S E . I N S T . E N G R
. T A K E T H E C A K E .
. L I L . R A F . . . . .
R A I N . Y E T . C E O .
O K S . C H A O S . L M N
B A T . A O K . F A T E .
. . O A T . P I P . . . .
. D O W N T O E A R T H .
W A V E . U P I N . R A E
O L I N . B E N D . A L L
K E D S . N E A . P T S .
```

Puzzle 4

```
B O B . M A S . . D I V A
L I L . E M I T . O V E N
E L A S T I C S . D E E D
U S H E R S . H U G . . .
. O O H . I N E P T . . .
P E R U . M R I . L I D .
E V E L . C R T . R O L E
G A P . M A T . A T T N .
. S O L A R . R S T . . .
. . E A R . E L O I S E .
U S D A . O R I E N T E D
M O O D . T U N E . E G G
A X I S . T S P . M A Y .
```

Puzzle 5

Puzzle 6

Puzzle 7

Puzzle 8

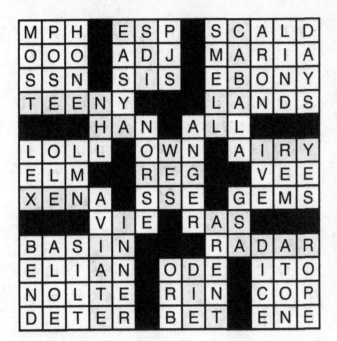

Puzzle 9

Puzzle 10

Puzzle 11

Puzzle 12

Puzzle 13

Puzzle 14

Puzzle 15

Puzzle 16

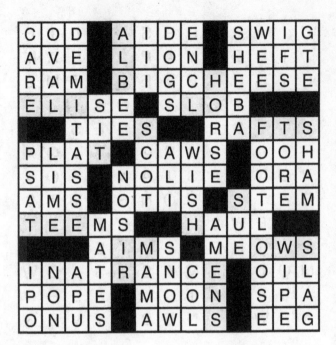

Puzzle 17

Puzzle 18

Puzzle 19

Puzzle 20

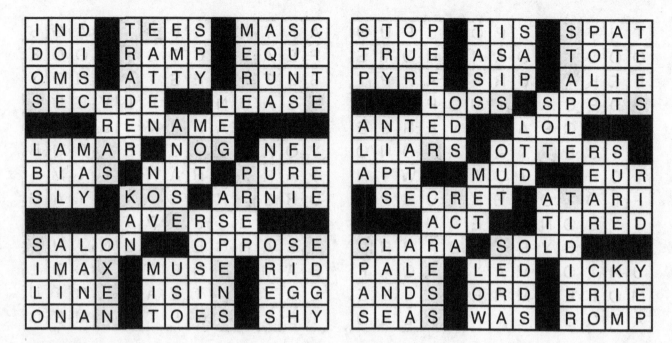

Puzzle 21

Puzzle 22

Puzzle 23

Puzzle 24

Puzzle 25

Puzzle 26

Puzzle 27

Puzzle 28

Puzzle 29

T	W	O		S	C	A	B		G	A	S	P
R	A	P		T	A	M	E		A	C	H	Y
E	D	U		R	I	C	E		T	E	A	R
Y	E	S	S	I	R			M	E	R	G	E
		A	P	O	L	L	O					
U	N	T	I	E		E	A	S	I	E	S	T
P	E	N	N		I	V	Y		N	O	N	O
S	A	N	T	A	F	E		M	E	N	L	O
			D	I	E	T	E	R				
D	I	T	T	O		R	A	T	T	L	E	
E	G	G	O		C	L	O	G		I	I	I
L	O	I	N		E	A	V	E		V	A	N
A	R	F	S		O	P	E	R		O	M	S

Puzzle 30

B	R	A	T		S	A	M		S	A	I	D
L	I	T	E		O	X	O		L	I	M	A
T	O	M	S		N	E	D		A	R	U	T
			T	A	G			N	Y	S	E	
L	A	S	E	R	S		L	O	G			
A	N	O	D	E		G	O	T		T	W	A
O	K	S		T	O	A	S	T		R	I	G
S	A	O		O	W	L		A	T	O	N	E
		R	O	N		S	W	E	D	E	S	
N	O	T	E		N	A	N					
E	A	R	S		R	O	E		S	E	M	I
W	H	E	E		A	L	E		E	W	A	N
S	U	E	T		P	E	R		S	E	E	D

Puzzle 31

K	I	M		A	B	C	D		C	H	I	T
I	C	Y		B	A	S	E		H	U	S	H
D	A	N		U	R	I	S		O	H	M	Y
	N	A	B	S		I	F	S				
		L	E	T	S		B	E	A	S	T	
U	P	T	O		H	O	P	I		W	O	O
S	E	A	T		I	F	I		L	E	A	N
P	A	T		G	N	A	T		I	S	P	Y
S	K	E	I	N		S	A	K	E			
		C	U	P		O	U	S	T			
U	N	D	O		U	C	L	A		H	E	W
N	O	O	N		M	A	U	L		U	N	O
I	N	N	S		A	L	G	A		N	N	W

Puzzle 32

C	R	Y		G	Y	M	S		S	P	F
O	K	E	D		R	E	A	L		P	I	E
G	O	T	O		I	N	T	O		U	P	S
		L	T	D		O	G	R	E	S		
S	M	I	L	E		R	A	P	S			
L	A	S		A	P	E	X		A	I	M	S
U	Z	I		R	U	L	E	R		N	A	H
M	E	N	U		N	A	D	A		C	U	E
		S	T	Y	X		T	R	A	I	L
A	L	I	C	E		D	E	Y			
M	I	C		N	U	D	E		A	R	C	H
F	E	B		D	R	E	W		N	O	P	E
M	U	M		S	L	A	Y		W	R	Y

Puzzle 33

Puzzle 34

Puzzle 35

Puzzle 36

Puzzle 37

Puzzle 38

Puzzle 39

Puzzle 40

Puzzle 41

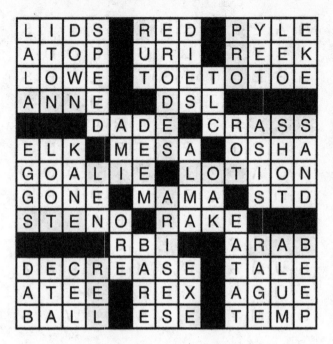

L	I	D	S		R	E	D		P	Y	L	E
A	T	O	P		U	R	I		R	E	E	K
L	O	W	E		T	O	E	T	O	T	O	E
A	N	N	E			D	S	L				
		D	A	D	E		C	R	A	S	S	
E	L	K		M	E	S	A		O	S	H	A
G	O	A	L	I	E		L	O	T	I	O	N
G	O	N	E		M	A	M	A		S	T	D
S	T	E	N	O		R	A	K	E			
		R	B	I			A	R	A	B		
D	E	C	R	E	A	S	E		T	A	L	E
A	T	E	E		R	E	X		A	G	U	E
B	A	L	L		E	S	E		T	E	M	P

Puzzle 42

M	R	S		G	O	D		B	R	A	S
R	O	W	S		A	T	E		R	O	I	L
E	M	I	T		P	C	S		I	N	D	Y
D	E	M	O	T	E		C	U	T			
	L	E	S	S	E	R		P	R	O		
S	A	L	E	M		U	N	I		R	A	P
A	V	O	N		H	I	T		L	I	Z	A
C	I	A		W	E	T		C	A	M	E	L
S	S	N		A	R	E	N	O	T			
	S	H	E		E	D	I	T	O	R		
F	R	A	U		T	O	W		N	A	N	U
H	A	V	E		I	R	E		O	R	E	S
A	H	A	S		C	A	R		P	S	T	

Puzzle 43

O	D	S		A	S	S		S	H	O	P
R	O	T	S		T	N	T		A	E	R	O
S	E	N	T		M	O	O		R	E	E	L
		A	R	S	O	N		A	D	O	S	
H	A	S	T	E		P	E	E	N			
A	P	L	U	S		S	S	N		A	N	D
R	E	U	S	E			C	A	N	O	E	
M	S	G		A	R	R		A	R	T	I	E
		A	T	E	E		S	E	E	R	S	
A	P	T	S		A	L	L	E	N			
N	O	A	H		C	O	O		A	S	A	P
N	O	S	E		T	A	N		S	A	T	S
A	R	K	S		S	D	I		C	O	T	

Puzzle 44

A	D	D		A	L	S	O		N	A	P	A
L	E	I		R	E	E	D		A	L	E	C
L	E	S	S	E	N	E	D		S	P	A	T
		N	A	T	S		F	A	S	T	S	
S	E	M	I	S		T	E	L	L			
A	R	I	D		P	O	L	E		P	O	P
C	I	N	E	M	A		K	A	R	A	T	E
S	C	I		B	I	A	S		H	A	I	L
		H	A	R	M		M	O	R	S	E	
R	A	K	E	S		E	G	A	D			
O	M	N	I		A	L	A	N	A	L	D	A
A	B	E	S		R	I	S	E		C	O	N
D	I	E	T		C	A	P	S		D	I	G

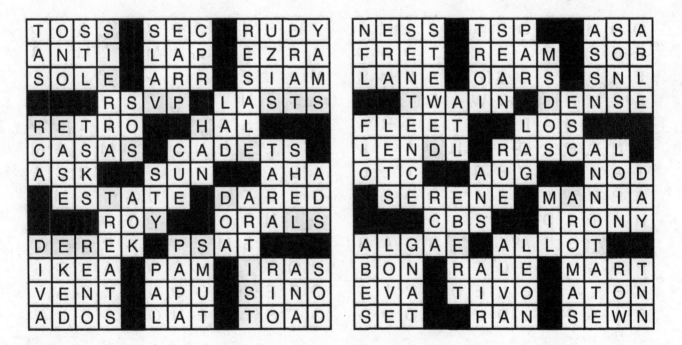

Puzzle 45

Puzzle 46

Puzzle 47

Puzzle 48

Puzzle 49

Puzzle 50

Puzzle 51

Puzzle 52

Puzzle 53

P	A	T	E		M	A	C			O	F	F	S
O	W	E	D		T	H	U			R	A	L	E
S	A	N	G		V	A	T			G	N	A	W
H	Y	D	E			B	E	L	A				
			S	O	D			I	N	T	R	O	
C	I	D		R	O	U	S	T		Y	A	P	
U	Z	I		I	N	G	O	T		P	I	E	
B	O	N		E	T	H	Y	L		O	L	D	
A	D	O	R	N		S	E	A					
			E	T	C	H		N	U	M	B		
C	H	O	P		L	O	G		T	R	E	Y	
H	A	D	A		O	H	M		I	S	N	T	
I	N	D	Y		D	O	T		C	A	S	E	

Puzzle 53

Puzzle 54

S	T	A	B		T	K	O			A	P	O	P
H	O	S	E		R	A	M			B	E	A	R
H	O	P	E		I	N	S			S	A	F	E
			T	U	B	E		M	E	S	S	Y	
P	S	A	L	M		F	I	N					
B	O	R	E	S		P	A	S	T	E	L		
S	T	U		H	U	T			U	A	W		
	S	T	O	P	I	T		L	O	R	N	E	
		R	E	P			S	M	O	K	E		
L	A	L	A	W		L	O	D	E				
O	B	I	T		B	O	W		L	I	S	A	
E	L	L	E		B	A	N		E	G	A	D	
B	E	T	S		C	D	S		T	O	G	O	

Puzzle 54

Puzzle 55

N	U	T	S		S	A	S	H		D	E	L	
O	P	A	L		C	H	I	A		A	L	I	
N	I	T	E		A	M	P	S		R	I	P	
	N	E	E	D	L	E		C	E	E	S		
		P	R	E		D	A	H					
P	R	O	S	E		H	O	S	A	N	N	A	
T	O	W		S	W	I	S	S		A	S	P	
A	T	L	A	S	E	S		A	T	P	A	R	
	N	Y	E		N	I	H						
R	A	P	S		S	A	L	O	N	S			
A	L	A		T	R	A	M		M	E	A	L	
I	V	Y		R	O	V	E		A	M	M	O	
D	A	S		I	D	E	S		S	O	S	O	

Puzzle 55

Puzzle 56

F	A	R		S	T	U			S	N	O	B	
I	I	I		T	E	R	I		P	A	L	E	
R	N	S		A	N	N	S		O	P	E	N	
S	T	E	E	R	S		A	R	R	E	S	T	
		L	E	E		I	K	E					
A	H	M	E		M	A	O		M	C	S		
I	M	A	C		B	A	H		H	A	D	A	
M	O	D		P	O	P			I	T	S	Y	
	K	O	S		H	O	R						
S	L	A	N	T	S		A	N	E	M	I	A	
N	I	L	E		E	D	I	T		A	R	M	
I	A	T	E		S	E	T	A		R	O	E	
P	R	O	S			S	I	P		C	N	N	

Puzzle 56

Puzzle 57

Puzzle 58

Puzzle 59

Puzzle 60

314

Puzzle 61

```
GSA . . IFS . . MEW
RENO . COO . SAVE
REDALERT . PIER
. SID . RINSE
ELSIE . PHAT
REPS . EUREKA
SAC . LATHE NOD
DAKOTA . LONI
NOEL METES
LIMIT . RAG
USAF ALACARTE
TIRE SUP LEIS
ETC SGT CEL
```

Puzzle 61

Puzzle 62

```
LIED PBS BESS
EAVE LOU ALEG
AMES ASP SLAT
ASIANS TARS
RTE ONE
SPREE GRE AGE
TIE ANTES PIE
DAM SUE THESE
SET ALA
SADE LEERAT
PURE EAT ARID
ATAD BIN SEND
ROWS BRA SAYS
```

Puzzle 62

Puzzle 63

```
IDS CAB SHAH
REC AXLE COPA
EMU CITE AWAY
IDAHO YODEL
LEM ONS
RBIS TRU DUO
EYEOFTHESTORM
GER REO ISIS
KAN DUD
ABATE ONEAL
STAR TANS LED
ROLE SHOE EEE
SPIN ARR CRY
```

Puzzle 63

Puzzle 64

```
USE TOFU SASS
MIA ITON TWIT
PCT MISO EENY
EPICS LEDGE
ACRID IBID
PAIN CLOT OUR
PRESTO LEANTO
TDS HALT DEAD
RALE TITHE
SANER ECONO
LION EWOK OPT
ODIE RACE NAH
GERE RYAN EMU
```

Puzzle 64

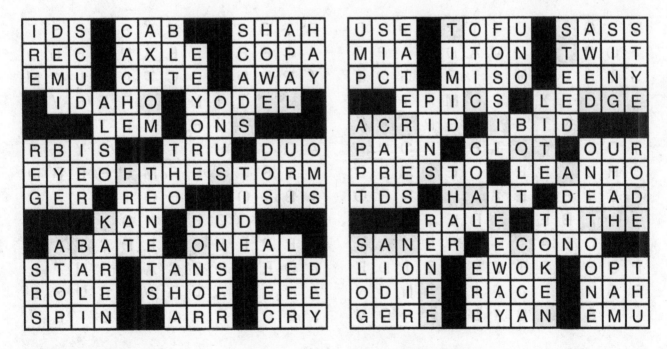

Puzzle 65

```
T A O S   M D S   I B M S
U N I T   O O H   N O E L
T A L E   D D E   S W A Y
U S S R   O S A Y
    N O T   S N A F U
A S T O R I A   S C R A P
S K A   T E A S E   L I T
P I X I E   H A N S O L O
S T I N G   G T O
    L A Y S   A N E W
N I C E   M I D   R O M E
P O E T   C P U   E V I L
R U E S   A S H   D A R T
```

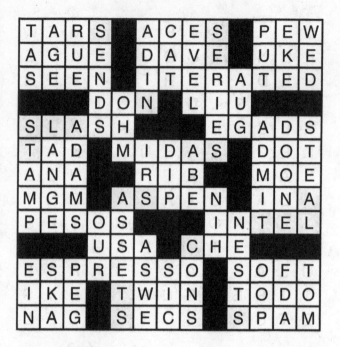

Puzzle 66

```
T A R S   A C E S   P E W
A G U E   D A V E   U K E
S E E N   I T E R A T E D
      D O N   L I U
S L A S H   E G A D S
T A D   M I D A S   D O T
A N A   R I B   M O E
M G M   A S P E N   I N A
P E S O S   I N T E L
    U S A   C H E
E S P R E S S O   S O F T
I K E   T W I N   T O D O
N A G   S E C S   S P A M
```

Puzzle 67

```
M S G   D I T   M U D
T O P   N O M A D   A P O
S T A L E M A T E   G O T
    E X E C   M A I N E
A G E N T S   S U P
T O D D   T E R R O R
O R D   P E N C E   M E D
    E Y E L E T   I N D O
    B E G   R E L I S H
S C U B A   B A W L
P O R   S T E P A S I D E
R E N   E A T I N   N U N
Y D S   B A D   N O V
```

Puzzle 68

```
R I G S   I R K S   P S T
A C R E   R E A P   E L O
T E R N   O C T A   L A M
    T I N   R E E V E
R A H   C H A L E T
A G O   H O L E   C Y A N
V E S T   R P M   H E R O
I S T O   S H O T   L A D
    O C E A N S   L B S
A P P L E   L P S
J O E   D E C A   I N T L
A N G   A V O W   R U S E
X E S   R A G S   S T E N
```

Puzzle 69

```
M R T   P G A     C H O P
S U E   R E T D   L O B E
G T E   O N M E   E R I C
    T U N E   C R A N E S
C R E P E   S L I T
O U R S   E L A P S E S
D D E   S N O R E   L I U
  E D U C A T E   D E N S
    T A C H   D A M E S
A S S O R T   B A B E
L O O P   E C O N   N P R
M I N I   D O N T   T A N
A L G A   W O E   S H A
```

Puzzle 70

```
A M Y S   A S P   S M U G
D U E T   D O A   T O R I
A L L A   J A N   R A G S
M E L B A   P E T I T E
    L U G   L I V
I L L E G A L   P E A R L
B E E   B B C   C O O
M O T E L   S A L I E N T
    L A B   D O C
  I M A G E S   N I C E R
I S I T   R E N   E L M O
N O N E   R A T   S U M O
A N D S   A S H   T E A K
```

Puzzle 71

```
B I D   R A P T   E E L S
A W E   O B E Y   S M U T
L A B   B E E N   T U G S
I S T O     P E T E
    N B A   A E S O P
S T R E E T C A R   P L O
P O E   A M O N G   A D S
O R D   T E N N E S S E E
T I D A L   A T A
    B E T A   W A I T
S T A Y   A V I D   N O R
L O W S   C O D E   T W I
O W L S   T W O S   S A M
```

Puzzle 72

```
D R I P   R U B   B L A B
R O B E   I S A   A I R E
U S E R   L O S   T E R A
M E T T L E   S H H
    A D D E R   C O M
M E L O N   A T S T A K E
I W I N   O R S   E V E N
S A L T I N E   D E E D S
T N T   N A S T Y
    J A N   R E L A T E
S A M E   D R Y   A H O Y
P T A S   O B S   I S L E
F L I T   N I T   T O D D
```

Puzzle 73

Puzzle 74

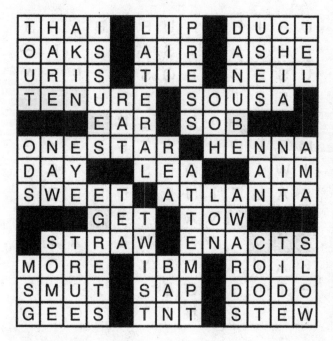

Puzzle 75

Puzzle 76

Puzzle 77

Puzzle 78

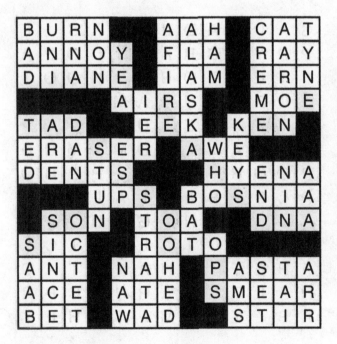

Puzzle 79

Puzzle 80

Puzzle 81

```
DESI   IWAS   RIP
ICES   NASA   AAH
TOTE   TRIB   YTD
     ERR   LOSES
LOL   NAUSEA
AGO   ANNE   FRAT
DRNO   SIN   SILO
DEEP   ITSA   LEM
     ESTEEM   EXE
APACE    LYE
BAT   CASE   LIED
UNO   TKOS   MONA
TEN   SAWS   SUES
```

Puzzle 81

Puzzle 82

Puzzle 83

Puzzle 84

Puzzle 85

Puzzle 86

Puzzle 87

Puzzle 88

Puzzle 89

Puzzle 90

Puzzle 91

Puzzle 92

Puzzle 93

Puzzle 94

Puzzle 95

Puzzle 96

Puzzle 97

Puzzle 98

Puzzle 99

Puzzle 100

324

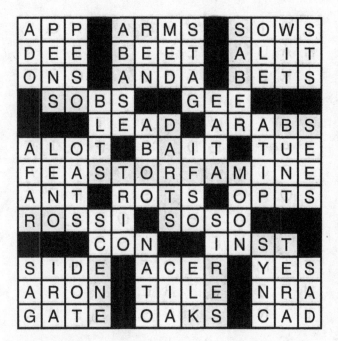

Puzzle 101

Puzzle 102

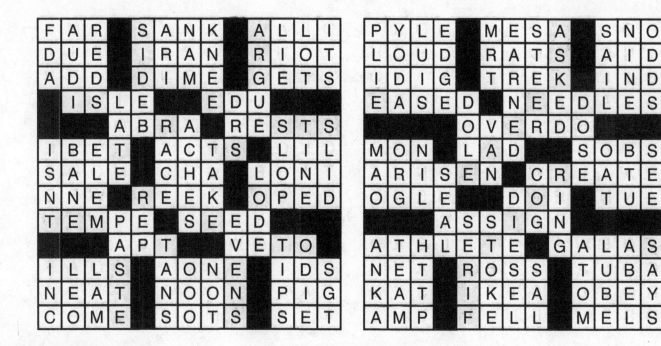

Puzzle 103

Puzzle 104

Puzzle 105

Puzzle 106

Puzzle 107

Puzzle 108

326

Puzzle 109

Puzzle 110

Puzzle 111

Puzzle 112

Puzzle 113

```
P H D . . . R E M . . W A S
C O O S . . O L D . S H I P
T E N T . . U M S . T E R A
. . O C T O . W R E S T . .
G A L O R E . M O E . . . .
E X A L T . B R O W S E . .
M I S . . H I S . . C A W .
. S T A T I C . T R A C E .
. . M I D . L O A T H E . .
. I S L A M . R A P T . . .
S U E Z . P I P . . E M M Y
P I N E . . J O E . D E A R
Y T D . . S T L . . N O S .
```

Puzzle 114

```
T A C . A D A M . . I N C A
H U E . L E G O . . D E L I
I N D . O W E D . . L A U D
S T E I N . . . P E R E S .
. A G A T H A . . . . . . .
B E A M . W O E S . . I C H
A R M . S A N D S . . T O E
A R I . O R I G . P A L S .
. R E C E S S . . . . . . .
S T A R T . . . M I T T S .
H O B O . A I R E . B O P .
I G O T . P E E L . S D I .
P O O H . B R A T . P O T .
```

Puzzle 115

```
I N N S . L A S . F E T A
S O O T . A L T . I N A N
A L S O . P L Y . E G G Y
Y O Y O . Y E A S . . . .
. G A G . S T I R S . . .
S C E N I C . T A B O O .
O I L . G N O M E . I V Y
F L A R E . D E R I D E .
T O W E L . D N A . . . .
. C A S S . . G L O P . .
F I N E . U K E . R A K E
C O E D . R I M . E D I T
C U B E . E D U . E Y E S
```

Puzzle 116

```
M A N . A C C T . R A S P
O N A . P A A R . E L I A
P A T . P L I E . D E R N
. S O R E . N E S S . . .
. R A T . S K E T C H . .
H A S S L E S . Y A H O O
O R A . E A T . . A N N .
S I S S Y . L I C E N S E
S A H A R A . N E E . . .
. T S P S . A L A S . . .
A L L I . A L P S . S O S
H E A R . R O L E . I N A
S A N E . T W O S . A G O
```

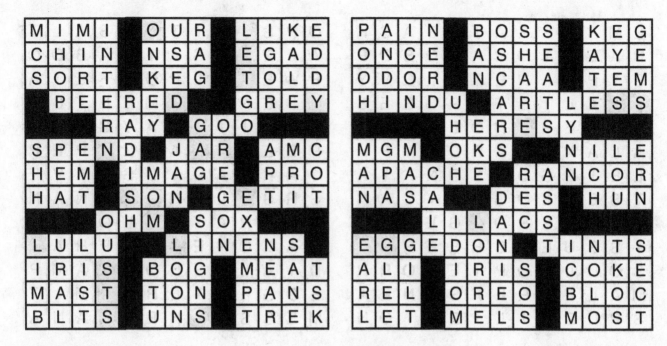

Puzzle 117

Puzzle 118

Puzzle 119

Puzzle 120

Puzzle 121

```
E M S  ·  S E A T  ·  S A C K
R A E  ·  T O R A  ·  O B O E
S T P  ·  A N E T  ·  L E V Y
 ·  A L I S T  ·  R O S E S
S O R E R  ·  H O E S  ·
A L A N  ·  L A R D  ·  M P H
L E T S G O  ·  S O N A T A
T S E  ·  L O G O  ·  I C A N
 ·  R E P O  ·  G L A S S
I S S U E  ·  S H E E R  ·
S O U L  ·  O P I E  ·  O R R
M A L E  ·  R E F S  ·  N E A
S P U D  ·  I L I E  ·  I O N
```

Puzzle 121

Puzzle 122

```
O P S  ·  B I T  ·  S A L T
W E T  ·  L S A T  ·  A B O O
E W E  ·  A L P O  ·  F E T A
 ·  S E N S E  ·  M E E T S
 ·  L I T  ·  R A Y S
P E E N  ·  A T E  ·  P E P
J A R  ·  A D I O S  ·  A V E
S R S  ·  L E N  ·  O N A N
 ·  R A T S  ·  L O O
 ·  A L O N E  ·  C A P R A
D I A L  ·  S H O W  ·  A M P
E D G E  ·  T E R N  ·  M I T
M E S S  ·  H E S  ·  A N A
```

Puzzle 122

Puzzle 123

```
D A D  ·  N O S  ·  P L U G
D A N A  ·  O N T  ·  H E R O
T H A T  ·  R E A  ·  A I L S
 ·  R E M I T  ·  S A S H
R O B I N  ·  L U B E  ·
A M O U R  ·  L E A  ·  P O P
F E R M I  ·  S T O P S
T N N  ·  C B S  ·  S A K E S
 ·  T O R A  ·  E V E N T
D I C E  ·  E L I T E  ·
R O A R  ·  N O T  ·  R S V P
O W N S  ·  D O S  ·  N E A R
P A T E  ·  A N Y  ·  P L Y
```

Puzzle 123

Puzzle 124

```
S L A M  ·  O N T  ·  C I T Y
C O C O  ·  D U H  ·  A C N E
A B C D  ·  O N E  ·  R U N T
M E T E O R  ·  R E D  ·
 ·  I S L E S  ·  L O P
B A S I L  ·  S I T U A T E
O R E L  ·  I A N  ·  S N I P
R E E L E C T  ·  P E A C E
N A N  ·  V I S T A  ·
 ·  S A N  ·  I N S E T S
P F F T  ·  E A T  ·  O B I E
O D I E  ·  S P A  ·  L A L A
T A R P  ·  S U N  ·  D Y E S
```

Puzzle 124

Puzzle 125

```
W I R E   C B S     N E W
E V E N   C A P   R I C H
T A B S   C R O   A C H Y
S N A I L     R O D E O S
      G A Y   T W I
A B A N D O N   L I G H T
S A P     U P S     U A W
H A B I T   R O M A N I A
      D A B   W I T
I N D I G O     T O P I C
N E R O   N H L   M A D E
C H E T   G E E   I R O N
H I D     O R G   C E L T
```

Puzzle 126

```
B R A G   W A R   A C I D
B A L E   W A D   S O D A
C Y S T   I R S   T R O Y
      S H I P   G U E S S
O R D E R     B E T
R O O T S   D E L E T E S
B U T     T O N     I S P
S T E P S O N   T A M P A
      R I M     O P E N S
S P L I T   S T Y E
H A R E   F L A   M E O W
E G O S   I O N   A L F A
L E N T   E G G   N I T S
```

Puzzle 127

```
M R S   S A F E   R A M A
A A A   U R I S   E X A M
N I L   P I E S   R I T E
E N T R E E   A M U S E S
      U R L   Y E N
S H E D     R E G   D D T
T U N E   R O D   M A Y A
L E G   N E B   A S E C
      S H H   R A G
C A T T L E   O L I V I A
A C H E   A H M E   I L L
R E A P   T I E R   S E P
A S I S   S P O T   A T O
```

Puzzle 128

```
  T O M   B A H   L C D
M E T A   E G O   O H O H
N A I L   D E M   R E P O
O S C A R   R E E N T E R
      I S H   A K A
A R I S T O T L E   O F T
B I D E   T W O   A U D I
C B S   S P I N A L T A P
      R I O   E P I
A C C O S T S   B A R G E
W H O A   A N D   S O O T
L I P S   T A R   E L E C
  C A T   O P S   S L R
```

Puzzle 129

```
MAS . LID . . SLUG
IVE . OTIS . PARE
MOT . NATE . AXLE
ENAMEL . END . . .
. DRY . REESES
BRASS . SEW . OYL
RIDE . PHD . CARA
IGO . LAY . SHREW
ESSAYS . PIE . .
. NET . ERRATA
ARTS . ETTE . NAH
CAVE . SKIN . IDO
TEAL . OTS . NAY
```

Puzzle 130

```
LAMB . ELS . DUPE
ONEI . LAT . ASIS
GOAT . AXE . DEPP
ENTERS . ANDRE
. TUT . KEY .
ANAHEIM . ALCOA
COLE . CCC . OUTS
TRIBE . SADNESS
. UPC . MEG .
SOLID . ENLIST
AWOL . REL . ETTE
HAZE . OXO . GTOS
ABET . MET . SOPH
```

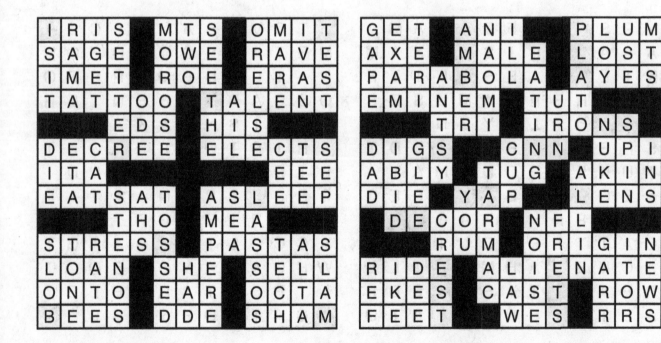

Puzzle 131

```
IRIS . MTS . OMIT
SAGE . OWE . RAVE
IMET . ROE . ERAS
TATTOO . TALENT
. EDS . HIS .
DECREE . ELECTS
ITA . . EEE
EATSAT . ASLEEP
. THO . MEA .
STRESS . PASTAS
LOAN . SHE . SELL
ONTO . EAR . OCTA
BEES . DDE . SHAM
```

Puzzle 132

```
GET . ANI . PLUM
AXE . MALE . LOST
PARABOLA . AYES
EMINEM . TUT .
. TRI . IRONS
DIGS . CNN . UPI
ABLY . TUG . AKIN
DIE . YAP . LENS
. DECOR . NFL .
. RUM . ORIGIN
RIDE . ALIENATE
EKES . CAST . ROW
FEET . WES . RRS
```

Puzzle 133

A	R	M	S		E	B	B		D	R	O	P
C	O	O	P		L	E	I		I	N	F	O
I	T	O	R		F	A	D		S	A	F	E
D	E	S	I			U	S	M	C			
			G	E	R		A	O	R	T	A	
A	I	D		N	E	O	N	S		U	R	I
W	H	O		C	A	R	A	T		T	O	N
L	O	N		O	L	D	I	E		H	I	T
S	P	E	A	R			R	R	S			
			G	E	T	S		T	A	P	E	
D	A	W	N		Y	T	D		A	L	A	N
O	P	I	E		P	O	D		R	I	N	G
S	U	N	S		O	W	E		S	E	E	R

Puzzle 134

H	A	I		S	N	A	P		A	L	U	M
U	R	N		C	I	A	O		S	I	N	E
B	C	D		A	P	A	L		N	E	S	T
	H	O	W	L		E	Y	E				
	H	A	R	T		E	R	I	E	S		
O	K	I	E		I	A	M	A		M	R	T
R	I	T	E	O	F	P	A	S	S	A	G	E
A	W	L		N	E	E	D		E	C	O	N
L	I	L	A	C		R	E	B	A			
	B	E	D			A	L	L	S			
G	O	R	E		E	M	I	T		A	U	G
M	O	A	T		N	O	N	E		S	L	O
T	O	M	S		T	O	N	S		H	U	T

Puzzle 135

I	T	B	E		S	T	N		S	T	D	
B	R	O	W		T	A	I		S	W	A	Y
M	I	N	I		A	C	T		N	I	K	E
S	O	O	N	E	R	O	R	L	A	T	E	R
			G	E	L		O	A	R			
Y	D	S		K	I	M		D	E	L	T	A
R	O	S	E		T	E	A		S	T	E	P
S	C	E	N	T		T	S	K		D	D	T
			G	A	S		S	E	A			
A	S	T	I	T	C	H	I	N	T	I	M	E
I	C	O	N		R	A	S		O	L	E	S
M	A	D	E		A	N	T		L	I	M	P
S	N	O		M	D	S		L	E	O	N	

Puzzle 136

T	A	N		C	A	P	O		A	G	O	G
H	U	E		A	S	E	C		S	O	L	E
A	T	M		M	I	N	T		T	R	I	M
N	O	O	N	E		A	T	H	E	N	S	
			F	R	I		L	E	M			
E	Y	E	L	A	S	H		E	A	G	L	E
P	O	T		M	E	W		T	A	D		
I	N	C	A	S		R	E	A	S	O	N	S
			V	A	T		D	N	A			
A	L	L	E	G	E		G	L	O	S	S	
T	I	E	R		M	I	R	E		S	C	I
I	M	E	T		P	O	U	R		H	A	T
P	A	R	S		O	U	T	S		A	B	S

Puzzle 137

T	D	S		T	S	A	R		M	A	I	M
V	E	E		A	T	N	O		E	R	M	A
S	A	T		S	A	Y	S		R	I	P	S
	T	O	T		E	M	C	E	E	S		
M	A	L	T	E	S	E		A	I	S	L	E
O	N	E	S		C	A	M	E				
B	A	S		A	T	A		S	I	D		
	T	R	E	K		T	O	R	E			
B	A	T	H	E		R	E	L	E	A	S	E
A	L	I	E	N	S		I	A	N			
L	O	A	M		A	W	E	S		D	A	H
S	E	R	A		C	O	O	T		S	K	I
A	S	A	N		S	O	N	S		O	A	T

Puzzle 138

C	L	I	P		A	S	K		S	L	O	P
N	I	N	E		B	A	A		P	O	L	O
N	U	K	E		B	I	N		E	G	G	S
	W	O	O	L		C	O	A	T			
A	L	B	E	R	T		W	A	S			
L	O	R	E	N		M	O	M		T	R	U
F	A	A		A	M	I	N	O		W	A	R
A	M	Y		T	A	X		R	E	I	G	N
	T	E	X		C	A	C	T	U	S		
R	I	P	E		B	E	L	L				
I	L	L	S		T	E	N		A	U	L	D
M	E	E	T		K	A	T		I	Z	O	D
S	T	A	Y		O	D	S		R	I	B	S

Puzzle 139

A	M	P	S		A	M	A		S	E	A	M
P	I	T	T		N	A	M		P	I	L	E
E	A	S	Y		N	A	Y		O	N	I	T
	L	I	E	N		P	O	S	T	S		
A	L	T	E	R		D	A	H	L			
T	O	A	D	S		P	O	D		S	L	O
O	R	R		P	A	L		C	O	W		
M	E	A		Y	A	K		P	L	A	T	E
	M	A	M	E		R	E	N	T	S		
S	T	R	A	Y		T	H	E	N			
L	O	U	T		A	T	A		S	O	L	O
A	T	I	T		F	L	U		E	Y	E	R
B	O	N	E		T	E	L		S	L	I	D

Puzzle 140

S	M	U	G		O	W	L		S	P	Y	
A	R	R	O	W		P	E	T		L	A	M
W	I	L	D	E		T	A	D		I	N	C
	T	O	I	L		M	A	A				
C	S	I		P	C	T		L	E	M		
O	O	D	L	E	S		H	B	O			
O	N	I	O	N		R	A	B	B	I		
	T	V	A		O	R	D	E	R	S		
T	A	T		P	E	W		G	A	P		
S	A	D		P	I	N	T					
O	H	M		R	E	G		I	R	I	S	H
P	O	E		P	A	H		M	O	T	O	R
H	E	N		M	R	T		M	O	B	S	

334

Puzzle 141

```
ARE  EATS  EUR
TELL THAT  MNO
OHIO HAIR  PET
NETTLE LARIAT
CAESAR PARSE
ERS SEEK  TEEN
    TALES
LANE LORE  IAN
AGILE ORANGE
PREFER SASSES
SEC RISE  PENT
EEE INAN  SADE
DDS EDGE  MAD
```

Puzzle 142

```
DATA PAC  LIND
AXED ALL  BOAR
SLED REASSURE
HEN POSSE  SCI
   ABEL  PAW
NEGATE SMARTS
OWES    SOLO
TERESA INTACT
   SOD  DEED
USC ROGET  RAF
SWEETPEA MAMA
DADS TEL  ICER
APES SRS  GENE
```

Puzzle 143

```
RTE  LSD  BAS
PUNT EMS  BACH
MEDIEVAL ARLO
  MAIL  ENSUE
POSER  LEIA
ANTI PENNAME
IMUS NOG  ANIN
REDMEAT  SONY
  OLGA  APNEA
SCANS TOLL
PATE TORTILLA
ARTY HEE  TOON
SPY  ESL  YON
```

We Have EVERYTHING® on Anything!

With more than 19 million copies sold, the Everything® series has become one of America's favorite resources for solving problems, learning new skills, and organizing lives. Our brand is not only recognizable—it's also welcomed.

The series is a hand-in-hand partner for people who are ready to tackle new subjects—like you!

For more information on the Everything® series, please visit *www.adamsmedia.com*.

The Everything® list spans a wide range of subjects, with more than 500 titles covering 25 different categories:

Business	History	Reference
Careers	Home Improvement	Religion
Children's Storybooks	Everything Kids	Self-Help
Computers	Languages	Sports & Fitness
Cooking	Music	Travel
Crafts and Hobbies	New Age	Wedding
Education/Schools	Parenting	Writing
Games and Puzzles	Personal Finance	
Health	Pets	